JOB

The Mystery Hidden in the Hebrew Pictures and Numbers

C.J. LOVIK

www.lighthouse.pub

Visit our website
to purchase books and preview
upcoming titles.

Contact us at:
feedback@lighthouse.pub

Copyright © 2019, C.J. LOVIK
All rights reserved

Cover Design and Interior Layout by Sergio E. León
Sergio was born and raised in Mexico City, where he studied Design and Arts in the National Autonomous University of Mexico (UNAM). For nearly 20 years, Sergio has worked in a variety of positions, primarily acting as Art and Design Director for major brands and publications. Today, Sergio is the Art and Design Director for Lighthouse Gospel Beacon, where he is responsible for all digital and print media. Every day, Sergio is growing in Christ while continuing to produce art and media to help illustrate the love of the Savior. Sergio is married to his wonderful wife, Monica, and they have two amazing children.

In what is likely the oldest chronological work in the Holy Scriptures, I invite the reader to follow this amazing journey through the book of Job, paying special attention to the beginning and ending of this divinely ordained work written for our edification.

It is at these two strategic points in the book of Job we uncover an amazing revelation that has been largely lost and misunderstood for thousands of years.

Using the conventional Ancient Hebrew that includes the pictures and numbers as a compass, we will discover True North from God's perspective. With our eyes opened by the light of God's word, we will discover the transformational truths that accurately reflect the character and purposes of God toward fallen man.

And of course, we will find the distinct shadow of the one figure that transcends all of Scripture—the Lord, the Author of our Salvation, the Beginning and the End—Jesus the Christ, our only hope for the world to come.

C.J. LOVIK

CONTENTS

CHAPTER 1
THE STORY OF JOB 6

CHAPTER 2
SATAN, HEBREW PICTURE MEANING 22

CHAPTER 3
SATAN'S KINGDOM, UNDER THE FIRMAMENT ... 30

CHAPTER 4
**SATAN IS NOT ALONE UNDER
THE FIRMAMENT!** 40

CHAPTER 5
DOES JOB'S NAME MEAN HATE? 52

CHAPTER 6
DOES JOB'S NAME MEAN ENEMY? 60

Chapter 7
DOES JOB'S NAME MEAN GRIEVING AND GROANING? 78

Chapter 8
THE MEANING OF JOB'S NAME 90

Chapter 9
HIDDEN MEANING REVEALED IN THE NAME OF JOB! 120

Chapter 10
JOB'S MISERABLE COMFORTERS 132

Chapter 11
THE REAL MEANING OF THE NAME OF JOB! 146

Chapter 12
GOD'S MYSTERY MIRACLE MATH 164

CHAPTER 1

THE STORY OF JOB

We are all familiar with the story of Job. But did you know that there is a prophecy in the name of Job that was specifically for Job but also for all those that Love the Lord?

Join me as we unravel the mystery hidden in the name and life of Job.

JOB 1:1

There was a man in the land of Uz, whose name was Job; and that man was perfect and upright, and one that feared God, and eschewed evil.

The epic battle for the soul of Job is a true story from beginning to end.

It is also an allegory that is meant to invite all those that love the Lord to take a balcony seat where we can observe with keen interest the drama that unfolds for our edification.

The story begins with what first appears to be a harmless commendation.

The ignition point that launches the story of Job did not take place on earth, it took place in God's Heaven above the earth where we are invited to listen in on one of the few conversations to ever be recorded from Heaven's glorious and mysterious location.

Pay close attention to the conversation between the Creator, Elohim, and the arch enemy of our souls, Satan.

JOB 1:8

And the Lord said unto Satan, Hast thou considered my servant Job, that there is none like him in the earth, a perfect and an upright man, one that feareth God, and escheweth evil?

Let's put this in modern parlance.

Imagine a board meeting.

Now imagine an ex-employee who has arrived at the board meeting as an unwelcomed and uninvited guest.

Instead of having security throw the guest out, the CEO goes over to the arrogant ex-employee and calmly points out the accomplishments of one of his favorite employees.

The estranged ex-employee, who was sacked for insubordination and disloyalty, listens with a smirk on his face that cannot conceal his disdain.

After listening to the high praise, the ex-employee snaps back at the CEO with a cynical response.

"You just gave him a big raise and bought him a new home, of course, he is loyal and faithful. Fire him without cause, take away all his income and kill all his children and he will curse you to your face."

Does this seem a little too edgy?

It shouldn't because this is the earthly equivalent of the Heavenly conversation that took place between God and Satan.

Not Like You!

We must not forget that the commendation of the faithful servant Job was also a pointed condemnation of the unfaithful servant Satan.

The praise of a faithful servant would bring a smile and rejoicing to anyone that loved our Heavenly Father. But it would be equally as disquieting, challenging and annoying to anyone that hated our Heavenly Father.

It is in this context that we hear the words of the Most High God spoken to Satan.

"Have you considered My Servant Job?"

Now consider the suffering and grief, death and destruction that will soon follow this Heavenly conversation, and then ask yourself how unlikely it is that there is a prophecy of Promise just waiting to be discovered in the name of Job.

Is this even possible?

Unlikely is never an obstacle for God as we are about to find out.

Let's take a look at the picture and number meaning of the name of Job as we look at the seemingly impossible promise that is prophesied in the pictures and numbers in the name of Job.

At this point, I would like to inform the reader that we will not be using the Modern Block Hebrew in this book. The Modern Block Hebrew came into use during the exile of Judah in Babylon about 500 years before the birth of Messiah.

Abraham, Isaac, Jacob, Moses, Joshua, Samuel and David would not have been able to read the Modern Hebrew Aleph-Beyt as all the letters were dramatically changed from obvious pictograms to obscure block letters that conformed to the Aramaic block letters popular in Babylon.

All the Hebrew words we will be exploring in this book will be presented as Early Hebrew Symbols. We will always put the name of the Pictogram for your convenience. In many cases, we will also include the Picture that the Pictogram represents. As you can see below, the connection between the Pictogram and the Picture are obvious in the Early Hebrew. That is not the case in the later version of the Hebrew Aleph-Beyt that sprang out of the Babylonian captivity.

To be clear…

Early Hebrew (below) and Modern Hebrew (above)
Remember that Hebrew is written from Right to Left

ALEPH

THE EARLY HEBREW PICTOGRAM

1

Will be substituted for
ALEPH

Modern Block Hebrew Script

1

TAV

THE EARLY HEBREW PICTOGRAM

400

Will be substituted for
TAV

Modern Block Hebrew Script

400

JOB • The Mystery Hidden in the Hebrew Pictures and Numbers

And so on for the rest of the 20 Pictograms contained in the Hebrew Aleph-Beyt.

Let's begin by taking a look at the Pictures and Numbers in the Hebrew name Job.

The final translation of the Hebrew Pictures and Numbers will not be disclosed until the final chapter. In the meantime, see if you can figure it out based on the meaning of each letter and number in the name of Job.

GOD THE FATHER

The first Hebrew letter in the name of Job is Aleph. Aleph is pictured as an OX and is meant to convey the meaning of the Strong Leader. The Hebrew letter Aleph is also the number ONE. Ideally, the person in view is God the Father.

The Mystery Hidden in the Hebrew Pictures and Numbers • JOB

Yood is pictured as a hand doing a deed. Yood, the number 10, is spiritually significant as it signifies a sequence of events Ordained in Heaven Unfolded on the Earth in order to accomplish God's purpose. The number 10 is the number of Divine Ordinal Perfection.

In other words, God has ordained a sequence of events in Heaven that will unfold perfectly on earth in order to accomplish His purpose.

Iron Nail, Wooden Hook
To secure two things together

Vav is pictured as an iron nail or a wooden hook that connects two things that are separated from each other.

Vav, the number 6, is the number of Man.

Beyt is pictured as a tent or a house.
Beyt is also the number 2.
The number 2 is a picture of the Son of God
the Second Person in the Trinity.

Can you figure out the picture and number meaning of the name JOB?

JOB

IS THERE A HIDDEN PROPHECY IN THE NAME OF JOB?

It is only by understanding the prophecy hidden in the name of Job that we can even begin to understand what the revelation we discover in the most ancient book to be placed in the prophetic text we call the Bible is all about.

This message will become clearer by the time we finish our study of the book of Job. It is a revelation that is as wonderous and important today as it was nearly 4000 years ago during the time of Job.

Things are not always as they appear and we should be cautioned by the story of Job not to ever be too hasty in predicting the outcome, understanding the circumstances or predicting the destiny of anyone who loves the Lord.

The Apostle Paul paraphrasing Isaiah the Prophet said it best:

> # 1 Corinthians 2:9
>
> *But as it is written, Eye hath not seen, nor ear heard, neither have entered into the heart of man, the things which God hath prepared for them that love him.*

Servant
Hebrew Pictures Meaning

The book of Job reveals the first time that God calls anyone My Servant. Is there a mystery hidden for us to discover in the Hebrew word Servant? You are about to find out.

It is commonly believed that the first book published and placed into the canon of Holy Scripture was the book of Job.

As we open the pages of the book of Job and read its pages, the first thing we discover is Satan showing up uninvited into the Courts of Heaven in God's Kingdom.

Satan is up to his eyeballs in schemes and full of deceit and has been busily going to and fro on the earth seeking whom he may devour.

God interrogates Satan. Satan is sly and does not own up to the mischief he has been creating on the earth. He only casually mentions that he has been going to and fro about his business as the presumptive prince of this world, his temporary kingdom.

Then when Satan least expected it, a prize is dangled in front of his eyes. An opportunity to express the evil desires of his withered heart shines like a precious jewel just within his reach.

Satan does not hesitate, he does not consider that perhaps the scheme upon which he so quickly pounces could fail. Satan's hubris and arrogance overwhelm all reason as his bloodlust drives him to damage and destroy anything that God has stamped with His Royal approval.

Satan seeks to bolster his own reputation at the expense of what he vainly imagines as God's naive assessment of "His Servant Job."

This is the perfect opportunity and one he has been pining for, the chance to put a visible dent in the Glory of God.

Satan relishes the opportunity to ply his stock and trade on unsuspecting Job.

Listen to what the Scriptures reveal in Job 1:8:

> ## JOB 1:8
>
> *The Lord said to Satan, "Have you considered My servant Job? For there is no one like him on the earth, a blameless and upright man, fearing God and turning away from evil."*

Considered Job?

Of course, Satan had considered Job.

Job was an irritation and vexation to Satan. It aggravated Satan greatly that God had built a hedge of protection around righteous Job.

The Mystery Hidden in the Hebrew Pictures and Numbers • JOB

There was no need for Satan to return to the earth to investigate the life of Job. If Job had committed any unrighteous acts upon the earth, Satan, the great accuser of the brethren, would have made that known to God in a flash.

Instead, we hear this response **Verse** from Satan.

"Take down the hedge of protection and stretch forth your hand and take away all his blessings and he will curse you to your face." Satan snarled.

"I will not do that" reported the Lord. "But I will allow you to do your worst against Job, except you must not take his life."

The challenge was taken up and relished by Satan who immediately rushed out of the courts of Heaven eager to begin doing his worst against the one man that God considered more righteous than any other man on the earth.

The one who God called, "My Servant Job."

SERVANT

The very first time we find the Hebrew word Servant is in Genesis 18:1-3. This is where we read the story of the Lord appearing unto Abraham to announce the soon arrival of the promised son.

> And the Lord appeared unto him in the plains of Mamre:
> and he sat in the tent door in the heat of the day;
>
> And he lift up his eyes and looked, and, lo,
> three men stood by him:
> and when he saw them, he ran to meet them from the tent door,
> and bowed himself toward the ground,
>
> And said, My Lord, if now I have found favour in thy sight,
> pass not away, I pray thee, from thy servant

SERVANT

| Reysh | Beyt | Ayin |
| 200 | 2 | 70 |

AYIN

TO SEE • KNOW • EXPERIENCE
TO UNDERSTAND

BEYT

THE HOUSE OR TENT
GOD THE SON

REYSH

THE PRINCE OF HEAVEN

The Mystery Hidden in the Hebrew Pictures and Numbers • JOB

The Picture meaning of Servant that we discover when we look at the hidden in plain sight revelation that God has placed at the root of the word is not what we expect to find.

This disclosure is meant to cause us to re-examine the concept and ultimate purpose of a servant from God's vantage point.

The dictionary defines servant as a person employed by another to perform duties, most often those duties are domestic.

The servant is the one person who is welcomed into the home in order to assist in the smooth management of the household.

The servant is not related to the master of the household but serves at his pleasure.

The Ideal Hebrew Word Picture paints a different picture.

Let's examine the pictographic meaning of each of the Hebrew letters.

Ayin, pictured as an eye, means to see, know and experience.

Beyt is pictured as a Tent or a House.

Reysh is the picture of the head person who in this case is the Prince of Heaven, the Son of God.

God called Job "My Servant."

Now let me ask you a question.

Had Job seen, known or experienced the Heavenly home of the Prince of Glory, the Son of God?

The answer is NO.

Does it follow that those who are God's servants here on earth will one day see, know and experience the hospitality of Heaven?

Job thought so.

Listen to what Job reveals in Job 19:25-27:

> *For I know that my redeemer liveth, and that he shall stand at the latter day upon the earth:*
>
> *And though after my skin worms destroy this body, yet in my flesh shall I see God:*
>
> *Whom I shall see for myself, and mine eyes shall behold, and not another; though my reins be consumed within me.*

Is God looking for domestic servants in Heaven?

Of course not.

What is God's plan for His servants here on earth?

The answer…God who called Job *My Servant,* would one day call Job His adopted son.

Job, a man, and always a creature, would none-the-less be adopted into the household of God.

Job's destiny is to be resurrected in order to one day call his Creator his redeemer and his Heavenly father.

What does this have to do with me?

Job's destiny is our destiny if we love God and have put our faith and trust in His only begotten son who came to undo the curse brought into the world by Satan and sin.

Listen to what John the Apostle speaking about Jesus, reveals in his Gospel account:

John 1:11-13

He came unto his own, and his own received him not.

But as many as received him, to them gave he power to become the sons of God, even to them that believe on his name:

Which were born, not of blood, nor of the will of the flesh, nor of the will of man, but of God.

CHAPTER 2

SATAN

HEBREW PICTURE MEANING

JOB 1:6-8

Now there was a day when the sons of God came to present themselves before the Lord, and Satan came also among them.

And the Lord said unto Satan, Whence comest thou? Then Satan answered the Lord, and said, From going to and fro in the earth, and from walking up and down in it.

And the Lord said unto Satan, Hast thou considered my servant Job, that there is none like him in the earth, a perfect and an upright man, one that feareth God, and escheweth evil?

Make no mistake; these words were designed as a challenge and a rebuke to Satan.

Satan did not miss the implications of God's question. It was a question that was designed to confront Satan with his own rebelliousness.

The words spoken by God to Satan were also understood as a challenge, exactly as God intended they would be.

Satan's Domain

It is in the created expanse above the earth and under the firmament called the "air" where Satan rules a host of angelic rebels and evil spirits.

It is from this perch that he makes it his frantic business to go to and fro on the earth looking for ways to advance his cause by making war against God's creation.

In order to fully understand the story of the trials and tribulations of Job, we need to discover the underlying revelation in the name of Job's Adversary.

Is there a hidden message in the Hebrew name we translate into English as Satan?

Understanding the hidden meaning of the name of Satan will help us get a vision of the story of Job, re-calibrated from a Heavenly perspective.

We all understand that Satan is our Adversary, the enemy of our souls.

But is there an additional testimony regarding Satan hidden in the Pictures that are embedded in the THREE HEBREW LETTERS that compose the name of Satan?

Let's take a look.

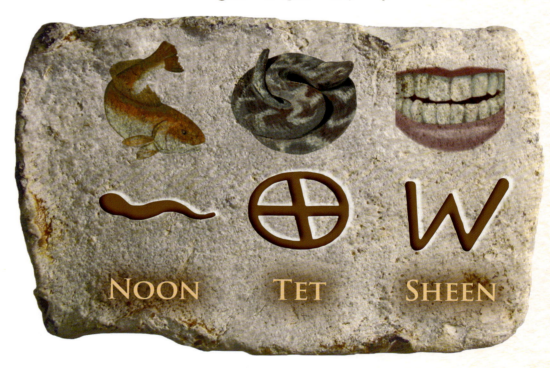

The Hebrew spelling of Satan is Sheen Tet Noon.

The first Hebrew Letter in the name of Satan is the letter Sheen.

Sheen is pictured as TEETH and it means to consume or destroy; it can also mean to press with sharp teeth in order to tear something apart.

The next Hebrew letter in the name of Satan is the letter TET.

TET is pictured as a SNAKE and means to Surround, to Twist, Entwine and Ensnare.

The final letter in the name of Satan is the Hebrew letter Noon.

Noon is pictured as a Fish and signifies activity and Life.

In conventional Hebrew, the word Satan is translated as THE ADVERSARY.

You cannot read the Biblical account of JOB without understanding that Job had an army of enemies on earth and in the Heavens that was directly above his head.

Who are these unseen enemies and why are they scheming and raging against us?

The purpose of this unseen kingdom is not a mystery to anyone who has opened up and read the ancient prophetic text that we call the Scriptures.

In this ancient book we call the Old Testament, we are told about an unseen kingdom that exists in close proximity to our own earth.

As we search the prophetic revelation we discover many things that are both puzzling and alarming. We learn that there is an invisible kingdom that is at war with the Creator and His creation, especially mankind.

The destiny of this kingdom ruled by Satan, including the prophetic declaration of its certain and soon demise, has not been hidden from us.

The destiny of the Prince of the Power of the Air along with all those that have sworn their allegiance to him willingly or unwittingly has been written as if it were history past.

In the meantime, the Dark Prince rages against the Lord God who made both Heaven and earth for reasons that are obvious to all those that believe God's Word.

In the Picture language, the Hebrew word Satan informs us as to the method and motivation of our Adversary Satan.

The Serpent that Surrounds and Ensnares us

Satan's goal is expressed in the letter Sheen

Satan desires to crush, devour and destroy.

And what is it that Satan wants to surround ensnare, crush, devour and destroy?

The answer is found in the Hebrew letter Noon

SATAN IS THE SERPENT THAT SURROUNDS AND ENSNARES US IN ORDER TO DEVOUR AND DESTROY OUR ACTIVITY AND OUR LIFE.

As a direct result of the disobedience of Adam, sin not only entered the world but it also entered into the hearts, minds and souls all the sons and daughters of Adam.

Each one of us struggles with the same rebellious spirit, hubris and arrogance that entered the heart and withered the spiritual life of the Cherub that once covered the throne of Almighty God.

Remember that Satan was privileged above all the other angels but instead of rejoicing in His Creator he coveted the praise and honor that is due God alone.

As followers of Yeshua, we are indwelt by the Holy Spirit of God. That does not mean we are beyond temptation.

What are we to do?

The Scriptures give us the answer.

1 Peter 5:6-8

Humble yourselves therefore under the mighty hand of God, that he may exalt you in due time:

Casting all your care upon him; for he careth for you.

Be sober, be vigilant; because your adversary the devil, as a roaring lion, walketh about, seeking whom he may devour:

Ephesians 6:12

For we wrestle not against flesh and blood, but against principalities, against powers, against the rulers of the darkness of this world, against spiritual wickedness in high places.

CHAPTER 3

SATAN'S KINGDOM

UNDER THE FIRMAMENT

Job is one of the most interesting and often misunderstood books in the entire Scriptures.

We will be examining the story of Job from a vantage point that is illustrated in the very pictures and numbers that make up the Hebrew words disclosed to us in the story.

The Lord has placed these pictures in the book of Job in order to increase our awareness of the hidden world that encompasses our daily lives.

In this book, we will examine the meaning of the Hebrew Word

Raqia (raw-kee-ah), the word we translated into English as Firmament.

Does this seem like a strange word to study as we explore the book of Job?

In our last chapter, we explored the Picture and Number meaning of Satan.

Do you know where Satan lives?

We know that he goes to and fro on the earth like a roaring Lion looking for more ways to create chaos and confusion, death and destruction.

But is that where Satan lives?

The answer is no.

Satan, our Adversary, temporarily dwells inside the FIRMAMENT.

Since this location plays an unspoken yet important part in the drama of Job, it would be a good place to investigate.

What is the Firmament?

Suspended between two realms, the earth, where man lives and the Heavens where God dwells, is a space under the firmament that is called Heaven, also known as the atmosphere and the air.

This is the realm where God placed the sun, the moon and all the stars on the fourth day of Creation.

GENESIS 1:14-19

And God said, Let there be lights in the
firmament of the Heaven
to divide the day from the night;
and let them be for signs, and for seasons,
and for days, and years:

And let them be for lights in the firmament
of the Heaven
to give light upon the earth: and it was so.

And God made two great lights;
the greater light to rule the day,
and the lesser light to rule the night:
he made the stars also.

And God set them in the firmament of the
Heaven
to give light upon the earth,

And to rule over the day and over the night,
and to divide the light from the darkness:
and God saw that it was good.

And the evening and the morning
were the fourth day.

We are told that one of the most important purposes of the firmament, where God placed the Sun, Moon and Stars, was to publish His amazing disclosure that reveals Glad Tidings to mankind. These are the "signs" revealed in Genesis 1:14.

The seasons in view are not just the four seasons of the year as we might imagine. They are the seasons that will unfold as pictured in the constellations seen circling over our heads at night in a repeating cycle that continues to this day.

It is a star-studded story of an epic battle followed by atonement and redemption that is repeated overhead, over and over again for our instruction.

It is a drama displayed in the Heavens in order to help man understand the good plans of our Creator.

The entire worshipful dance of the stars was designed for one purpose only. That purpose is to glorify God and announce the mission of His only begotten Son.

It is not a mistake, although the irony of it should not be missed, that Satan is banished to the very place where the Creator has placed the sun, moon and stars, His signs and His seasons.

Satan was cast into the Firmament, the very place that God created to display His glory.

Is it a surprise that Satan has perverted God's Heavenly revelation?

Was God surprised?

Hardly!

No matter how many myths and legends, false religions and pagan rituals depend upon the revised chaotic and perverted message that Satan has attempted to put forth to mask the truth, the truth does not change. The simple fact is that the Heavenly movement of the constellation has been purposely placed inside the Firmament as prophetic signs and harbingers that bear testimony to both the past and the future redemptive plans and purposes of God.

Satan may scramble the revelation of the constellations. He may try and make them scary and off-limits for Christians to consider.

The greatest liar and con-angel in the entire universe may conjure up a mythical mixed up message for the pagans and offer it up as secret occult knowledge.

Satan may then command those that believe his lies to view the Heavens, in which he is squatting, in order to obtain secret occult information.

All of this nonsense is meant to hide the true message that God put into the very design and constantly advancing parade of pictures that are displayed nightly in the Heavens.

None of Satan's lies can alter the fact that God named the stars and calls forth the constellation in order that those that love him might observe with confidence the story that finally ends under the victorious rulership of God's only begotten Son.

During the lifetime of Job and for almost half of human history, the only witness seen by the entire earth was the witness of the stars as they followed the pathways and completed the courses set by God.

When God showed up to have a face to face discussion with Job, He was very clear in what He revealed. God wanted Job to understand with certainty that "He" the Creator retained for Himself the glory due His name and He alone preserved the revelation He wants Job, and all of us to consider.

The Gospel that was first written in the Stars is the same Gospel written in the textual revelation so carefully preserved by God in order that we might know and love His truth.

God wants us to consider His redemptive work and has covered the earth with a Firmament, a Heaven directly above the earth that was designed from the very beginning to bear silent witness to His gracious plans, His power and His glory.

We should not be surprised that Satan would try and pervert that Glory. It must irk Satan considerably to be camped in a place that is teeming with bright celestial messengers that herald the power, might and wisdom of his greatest enemy.

It must be doubly irritating that the very Heaven in which he finds himself in his steady descent from God's Heaven above is the very place that publishes signs and heralds his own downward journey and ultimate demise.

It is more than interesting that we find numerous references to the signs in the firmament as we read the book of Job.

God points Job to the Heaven in order that Job might begin to understand that they are ever present to declare His Glory and that it is He alone that named the stars and brings forth the constellations in order to display His wise and wonderful plans for those that love and trust Him.

Now let's look at the Hebrew word Firmament.

Firmament is a word that in the Conventional Hebrew refers to the Heaven that is above the earth and the covering that arches over the entire earth and envelopes it like a dome.

I am sure you are curious what mystery is hidden in the picture meaning of Raqia, the word we translate as Firmament.

Let's take a look at the four letters that are also pictures that compose the Hebrew word Raqia (raw-kee-ah) that we translate into English as Firmament.

FIRMAMENT

| Ayin | Yood | Qoof | Reysh |
| 70 | 10 | 100 | 200 |

RAQIA

HEBREW PHONETIC SPELLING: (RAW-KEE'-AH)

The picture meaning of the Raqia (raw-kee-ah) or firmament, mentioned 9 times in the first chapter of Genesis is very instructive.

The picture and number translation is as follows:

The first letter in the word Raqia is Reysh pictured as the Head Person or the Prince.

The picture displays the True Prince of Heaven, the only begotten Son of God who is also the Creator.

The second letter in the word Raqia is Yood pictured as a hand doing a mighty work.

This pictures God's Divine accomplishment of Atonement and Redemption displayed in the Heavens.

This Divine Deed will be accomplished at the perfect time as ordained in Heaven in order that those that love God and are His children might have life that results in eternal fellowship with our Heavenly Father.

The third letter in the word Raqia is Qoof pictured as the back of the head. Qoof is the picture of the least and it is also the number 100. The number 100 tells us who God has in mind. The least in view are the chosen remnant, the children of promise. The easiest way to remember this is to bring to mind that Abraham was 100 years old when Isaac, the miracle child of promise, was born.

 The picture displays His Chosen People who are the least among all the other people of the world. The back of the head is to signify wandering and pilgrimage. We are pilgrims in this world, looking for a Heavenly city built by God.

The fourth letter in the word Raqia is Ayin, pictured as an eye.

 The picture means to See and Understand!

Ayin is the picture of those that see, know and understand.

They are the chosen children that will receive the promises of God.

Ayin is also the number 70.

Seventy is the number of the Nations. The revelation is easy to understand. God has chosen to reveal Himself and will call forth His remnant chosen people from all the nations of the world.

Representatives from all the nations both the Jews and Gentiles will ultimately be included in God's family.

Based on the pictures and numbers in the Hebrew word Raqia, let's summarize the hidden purpose of the Firmament.

THE TRUE PRINCE OF HEAVEN
THE ONLY BEGOTTEN SON OF GOD
WHO IS ALSO THE CREATOR.
DISPLAYS HIS DIVINE ACCOMPLISHMENT
OF ATONEMENT AND REDEMPTION
INSIDE THE FIRMAMENT
IN ORDER THAT HIS CHILDREN OF PROMISE
CALLED FROM EVERY NATION, TONGUE AND TRIBE
WILL SEE, KNOW AND UNDERSTAND THAT

HIS WORK OF SALVATION WAS ACCOMPLISHED BY THE ONLY BEGOTTEN SON OF GOD.

PSALM 19:1-4a

*The Heavens declare the glory of God; and the **firmament** sheweth his handywork.*

Day unto day uttereth speech, and night unto night sheweth knowledge.

There is no speech nor language, where their voice is not heard.

Their line is gone out through all the earth, and their words to the end of the world.

Now you know the hidden revelation in the Hebrew word

RAQIA

the word we translate into English as

FIRMAMENT.

CHAPTER 4

SATAN IS NOT ALONE UNDER THE FIRMAMENT!

A third of the angels believed the Fallen Cherub's slander and accusations against Elohim the Creator. These same rebellious angels were also cast out from the Heaven that is above the firmament.

Imagine a band of rebels who once enjoyed all the joys and preferments of God's eternal Heaven now cast away but not annihilated for reasons only completely understood by Elohim the Creator.

Is this an unsolvable mystery?

Instead of being destroyed they were banished and allowed to rule a kingdom directly above the earth and directly under the throne room of God Almighty.

Does this seem like a strange Divine strategy?

Could it be that the implications of this geography have enormous spiritual meaning for us?

Why not banish the rebels to some far distant place where they could not cause a problem for either God or man?

Obviously, God has a plan and purpose that only the evil one and his band of rebels can perform.

God has a purpose for Satan that impacts humanity in ways we do not normally consider.

Satan not only occupies space above the earth he is its temporary prince and ruler.

The same earth that God had created as a home for man has become the domain of Satan.

From the Heaven directly above the earth these dark angelic rebels have established a kingdom that is permanently occupied and busied with plans and schemes to destroy God the Creator and Man the pinnacle of God's creation.

What could be more fitting or delicious than to destroy the prized creation of your most hated enemy?

Satan must be wondering what God was thinking.

Consider that the circumstances Satan finds himself in would continually refill his cisterns with the poisonous venom of hatred. Satan was not "sent to his room" to cool off and think about what he has done. NO, Satan is given the opportunity to fully display for both God in Heaven, and man on earth, his own plans and purposes for God's creation.

Imagine a rage so fierce and constant that it has won you the rightly deserved reputation as the one who has come to kill and destroy.

Now imagine that you find yourself within constant range of your enemy's possessions.

Since God created man in His own image and placed him on the earth, what better place to establish your theater of operations? Imagine a battle zone directly above the earth. Isn't this the high ground that all adversaries seek in order to destroy their enemies?

What better target of blinding rage and unquenching malice than the creature man that God created in His own image and for Himself. What creature more deserving of sabotage and destruction than the creature lovingly created to experience fellowship with Satan's sworn enemy?

From Satan's point of view, the battle had gone well indeed. Armed with lies and deception and without resorting to physical violence, Satan has managed to send Adam the first man headlong into the path of death and destruction. With cunning skill, Satan managed to create a bitter rift between Adam's first two sons resulting in the elder brother killing the second born.

The first murder of a man was inspired by the Father of Lies who could now add homicide to his resume.

Satan had over time managed to send the entire population of the earth, a population that likely numbered in the billions, into a watery grave. Satan had orchestrated the vile unrelenting pollution of the earth so thoroughly that God was obliged to cleanse it with a catastrophic flood.

Can you imagine Satan chuckling to himself as he imagines that he has manipulated God into doing his dirty work?

Satan hates man. What better present could he give himself than the wholesale destruction of billions? What better outcome as a result of this watery catastrophe than untold billions of bodyless spirits that do not return to God because they do not belong to Him, hybridized by a Satanic Angelic Intrusion into the very DNA of mankind and no longer bearing any resemblance to God's perfect creation (Genesis 6)?

Imagine Satan's army swelling into the billions of newly recruited and willing evil Spirits full of malice ready to join the battle against God Himself and the pitiful creature called man.

All but a pesky remnant of 8 were unceremoniously removed from the earth with no further opportunity to repent and believe. Satan liked the odds, eight against billions. Remember that everything and everyone was lost except for a small righteous remnant that lived before the flood, and eight souls that remained alive after the flood.

Satan was going to have a heyday.

Did he?

The answer can be found in the valley of Shinar where almost the entire world present on the earth at the time gathered to make war against God the Creator.

The Prince of the Power of the Air and those on earth that owe allegiance to him marched against Job with a vengeance.

The Chaldeans and Sabeans who plundered Job's dwelling place and killed his servants were all willingly active human players in the assault on righteous Job. They were aided by an unseen angelic and demonic force that joined in common cause to mount an assault on Job's substance, servants and family.

The unrighteous are always eager to destroy and plunder the inheritance of the righteous.

Satan's complaint that Job had a hedge of protection around him would have been laughable if not so tragic.

Of course, God has a hedge of protection around his loved ones or else they would all be destroyed by Satan and his followers.

If we love the Lord then we are in a war with enemies both seen and unseen. If we love the Lord we are protected by Him in ways that may not always comport with our idea of "the victorious Christian life."

That does not mean we are not protected, and in the end saved from all the evil schemes and plans that Satan employs in order to keep us from entering God's Kingdom as beloved sons and daughters.

Listen to Satan's grievances against God.

Satan's complaint against God is proof positive of his single-minded arrogance, hubris and hatred.

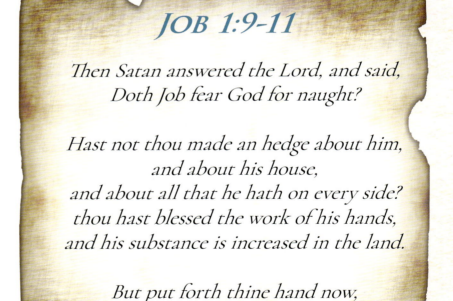

JOB 1:9-11

Then Satan answered the Lord, and said, Doth Job fear God for naught?

Hast not thou made an hedge about him, and about his house, and about all that he hath on every side? thou hast blessed the work of his hands, and his substance is increased in the land.

But put forth thine hand now, and touch all that he hath, and he will curse thee to thy face.

The fact that many of God's children seem blissfully unaware of their Heavenly Father's constant care and protection of them is shameful and should be repented of with constant prayers of gratitude.

We should be mindful of both His blessings and protection, whether it is seen or unseen.

God wants us to recognize His hand of protection in our lives, and although many times it is unseen it should never go unheralded.

Gratitude for the visible is wonderful, gratitude for the unseen is sublime!

With the hedge of protection removed, Satan would have completely destroyed Job. Had it not been for the commandment given by God that Job's life must be spared, Job would have been consumed by Satan's wrath.

It should be plain from the beginning that we are all in a battle. The outcome of this epic struggle will determine our eternal destiny.

Job lived a righteous and prayerful life within the well-defined boundaries of God's love and protection.

God asked Satan if he had considered His servant Job.

You can be certain that no one more aware of Job than his greatest enemy Satan.

If given the opportunity, Satan was certain that he could do the one thing that he did best. He could cause a permanent and irreparable division between Job and God.

Inside the Hedge of Protection!

Job lived on earth within the sanctuary of God's loving care and abundant blessings. Job was commended by God as the most righteous man on the earth at that time.

If Satan could destroy the relationship between God and Job, then there would be no man upon the earth that God could point to as true-hearted servant and friend.

If the most righteous man who loves and fears God can be turned into an enemy of God then the great adversary Satan has won a great victory and humiliated God.

If Job could be persuaded to abandon his faith and curse God to His face then Satan would be victorious.

The consequences of such an outcome would have shaken the very foundations of the Heavens.

Why Does God Allow Evil to Exist?

It is puzzling to many that God allows evil to exist in His created world. Mysterious, until you understand three simple truths.

The first thing to understand is that in the **past** evil did not always exist in God's Kingdom.

The second thing to understand is that in the **future** evil will one day be banished from Heaven and earth.

The third thing to understand is that the next time we are tempted to criticize God for allowing evil, we need to reflect on the fact that we were born into this world full of sin as a result of Adam's sin.

Each one of us does evil continually.

Sin by definition is evil, and sadly we are born with evil hearts.

Be Careful What You Wish For!

If God were to instantly remove all evil from the world, then you would no longer exist.

Remember that you are not a spectator in the drama between good and evil, you are a participant.

Sadly, without God's grace, we are all participants that would be taken out with the rest of the trash if we had our wish that all evil was instantly removed from the world we live in.

When the carnal man thinks for evil, he has in mind those things that are obstacles to his own happiness, plans and purposes. Anything that causes man pain or discomfort, among a host of other things, is then by definition evil.

God pronounces a verdict on this type of thinking. He calls it evil that proceeds from an evil heart. An evil heart, remember is our birthright as a result of Adam's sin and something we practice effortlessly every day of our lives.

Yes, evil is the problem.

But before launching forth on a campaign to eliminate it from the earth, you might want to take a look in the mirror of your own life and your own deeds, get off your high horse and pray for God's mercy. You might consider that God may have plans for dealing with evil that will one day be praised from the highest Heaven. Further consider that you and I, born and bred to sin, will be among the throng of redeemed and glorified creatures who were once entangled with evil and are now free from its bondage, free to bring praise and honor to the God who overcame evil in a way that we could never have hoped for or imagined.

Whenever I hear a "God hater" ranting about a God that "allows" evil and misery to exist I cannot help but be astonished.

Do they not realize that a world without evil is a world without them?

One day they will get their wish, all evil will be removed from the earth. What they fail to consider is that they will be removed with it.

In the meantime, God is restraining evil and using it to accomplish a purpose it was never designed to accomplish.

Only God can turn Temporary Evil into Eternal good!

Man has no idea how miserable and hopeless this world would become if He removed His gracious presence. The time is coming when He is going to do exactly that. It is going to be a short time that will last for only seven years. This is when those that dwell on the earth will get a lesson in evil that God Himself describes as something so terrible that the world has never seen anything like it.

So, we should probably think twice before we decide to lecture God on how He should manage His creation.

After all, God did not sin, we did.
God is not sinning, we are.

A little honest introspection and self-observation would produce instant humility and would be much appreciated by the management!

The truth is that God is using evil in ways we cannot understand in order to bring about something unimaginably good.

You say you can't see it?
Of course, you can't see it!

You're being tested in order to find out what kind of faith you have. Fickle faith that must be conjoined to instant results and visible signs at every moment. Or eyes that see what is not visible by faith, faith that both pleases God and will be justified by a reality so amazing that we cannot now imagine it, except by faith.

Since we are not in a position to know the mind of God, except what He has revealed, we are wise if we do not doubt but believe that all things including all the evil in the world will be used by our loving Heavenly Father to bring about something incredibly and eternally good for all those that love Him, yes, every single one of us.

Let's pause here and reflect on the Hebrew word that is translated into English as Enemy. We will be exploring this word in depth in a later chapter.

For now, there is just one thing I want you to notice.

Notice the third letter ✋ in the Hebrew word for Enemy is a picture of a deed done with the hand or arm doing a mighty deed. In the context of Satan, we know that the deed is being done is an evil deed.

Satan is the great Conductor of Chaos and Confusion and the Doctor of Death. He is a Thief and a Liar.

The mighty deed being done by Satan our adversary is not meant for our benefit but for our destruction. So, we can be assured that whatever deed Satan has planned, it is EVIL.

Yood ✋ the third Hebrew letter in the word we translate as enemy, is also the number 10 ✋.

The number 10 ✋ is one of 4 sacred numbers that means **Ordinal Perfection**. In other words, whenever we see the number 10 ✋ we are reminded and assured that whatever evil plans the enemy has in store for those that love the Lord, they will ultimately fail to produce the evil result Satan intended.

In our fallen corrupted condition, we do not even have the ability to see past the end of our nose, let alone anything close to an eternal vantage point. Since we cannot now see through eternal spectacles we are required to see with eyes of faith, things that cannot be seen in the natural.

No matter what it may look like to us, another greater supremely powerful work is being done on our behalf that guarantees an outcome that will ultimately unfold revealing something so good we cannot now imagine it.

This is the promise made to those that love God.

As we read the story of Job, we see the enemy at work doing his best to destroy Job.

Satan invited God to stretch out His hand and strike Job with adversity, but notice the Lord's response as recorded in Job 1:11-12:

JOB 1:11-12

...but put forth Your hand now and touch all that he has; he will surely curse You to Your face." 12 Then the Lord said to Satan, "Behold, all that he has is in your power, only do not put forth your hand on him." So, Satan departed from the presence of the Lord.

God allows Satan to test Job.

God removes the hedge from everything in Job's life that men hold dear.

Satan was given permission to touch Job's body; he was prevented from taking his life. Even if God had allowed Satan to take Job's physical life, there was one hedge of protection that would never be removed.

God loved Job and Satan could never take Job away from God, not even in death.

CHAPTER 5

DOES JOB'S NAME MEAN HATE?

Would you be surprised if I told you that the essence of HATE is revealed in the name of Job?

Bible scholars have speculated that the name Job means Hatred or Hated.

How they came to this conclusion is interesting and instructive.

To be clear, I am not saying, as some Bible scholars have speculated, that the name JOB can be translated as HATE or Hated.

Job clearly does not mean Hate or Hated.

But it does point you in that direction.

So, in order that you understand the true meaning of the name of the man that was caught up in a drama in which he was both a participant and a prize, a player and a pawn, let's investigate the idea that Job means Hated or Enemy.

If you do a search based on the KJV for the word **hate** you will be directed to Genesis 26:27.

The word translated hate in this verse should actually be literally translated as Hated and not Hate.

Actually, the first time the Hebrew word that is literally translated as HATE shows up in the Hebrew it is translated into English as Hated. This may seem a little confusing so let me see if I can clarify it.

The first mention of the literal Hebrew word HATE is found in Genesis 37:5 where we read the following:

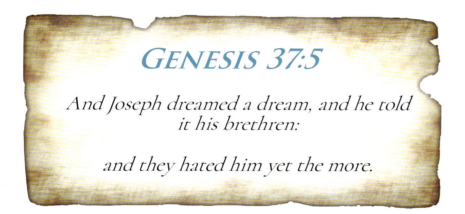

JOSEPH IS A TYPE AND SHADOW OF THE MESSIAH!

There are only two men in the Old Testament about which the Scriptures make no negative mention.

One of those men is Daniel and the other is Joseph.

Since all men are sinners, including the man Joseph, this oversight seems to be deliberate.

The reason for this omission has a messianic purpose.

The story of Joseph is the longest running narrative in the Old Testament. This is not surprising when you realize that Joseph was playing a part in real history that was meant to foreshadow the coming Messiah.

Joseph was rejected by his brethren and suffered untold miseries as a result of the hatred of his own flesh and blood.

Despite this rejection, it was Joseph who was the means of his brothers and their family's ultimate salvation in the natural realm.

Joseph, in the end, had the power to destroy his brothers who had acted with wicked malice toward him, without any consequences to himself. In spite of the natural reflexes of man to repay evil for evil, Joseph showed them uncommon mercy, love and grace.

In a hundred ways, ways we do not have time to explore in this book, Joseph was a picture of Jesus the Christ.

It is no accident that the first time the word Hate appears in the Scripture it is connected to the one person in all the Old Testament that was the most prominent shadow type of the coming Messiah.

If Joseph was a shadow type of Christ, then JOB is a shadow type of all those that truly love the Lord.

Job was born long before the Son of God was revealed as the Savior and Redeemer of the World.

That fact of history did not keep Job from seeing his Redeemer through the eyes of faith, and declaring with certainty that the means of his own resurrection and redemption was based on the Savior that he declared he would one day see with his own eyes.

We have this testimony in common with ancient, righteous Job.

We have not seen our Lord with our own eyes but believe with certainty that one day our faith will turn to sight and we will see with our own eyes the Savior who redeemed us and included us in His family.

As we examine the possible picture and number meanings of each of the three letters in the Hebrew word we translate as Hate, the meaning of the pictures will quickly become clear.

HATE

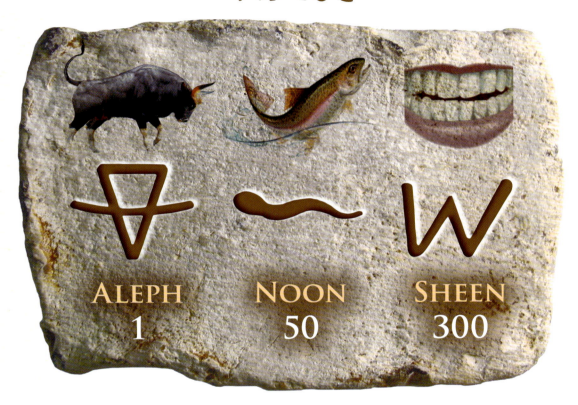

Let's take a look at the meaning of Hate starting with the first Picture in the first letter of Hate.

The first letter in the Hebrew word we translate, as Hate is Sheen W.

Sheen is pictured as teeth and it means to consume, tear apart and destroy.

CONSUME — DESTROY

The Mystery Hidden in the Hebrew Pictures and Numbers • JOB

The second letter in the Hebrew word we translate as **Hate** is Noon .

Noon is pictured as a fish and it means Activity and Life.

The third letter in the Hebrew word we translate as Hate is Aleph .

Aleph is pictured as an Ox and it means the Strong Leader.

The picture translation of Hate pierces to the heart of the malicious cancer of Hate as it unveils its true object.

Hate is a malicious desire that springs from the withered sinful heart of men, fallen angels and demons.

Hatred is the wellspring that brings forth violence, destruction and death.

Hatred is the contagious disease that infected Satan.

Satan understands the powerful forces of evil and rebelliousness that manifest when hatred is released. Satan is an expert at fanning the flames of man's complaints into a firestorm of hatred and directing it upward to Heaven.

The Picture meaning of Hatred is as follows:

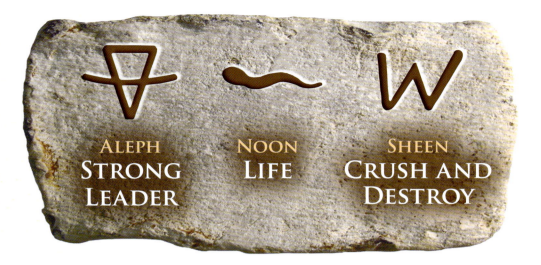

Aleph	Noon	Sheen
Strong Leader	Life	Crush and Destroy

To Crush and Destroy Life created by God the Father!

Hate, in the most ideal sense, is the desire to Crush and Destroy the Life and Activity of our Heavenly Father.

Hatred is a double-barreled shotgun, each shell loaded with a thousand complaints aimed at the Creator.

Hate had its beginning outside of our earthly realm.

Hate first appeared in Heaven and in the most unlikely place.

Hate was first found in the heart of an angelic Cherub who was the most privileged creature in all of Heaven. The hate that took root in the heart of Satan soon infected one-third of the angelic hosts.

What was the object of this malicious hatred?

The object was God, Himself.

Satan desired to imitate, replace and ultimately destroy God.

With that evil ambition ruling his withered heart, what better place for Satan to aim his hatred than God's creation.

Within that creation, what creature stands out as the perfect target for Satan's hatred?

Obviously, the creature that God loves the most.

And what creature is that?

The answer is Man, the pinnacle of God's creation.

Man is the one and only creature that we are told was created in His own image.

Satan is come to kill and destroy and we on our own are powerless to stop him.

There is only one remedy for hatred and it is Jesus the Christ who has both described the problem perfectly and offered Himself as the solution to all those that put their faith and trust in Him and Him alone.

Listen to the words of Jesus:

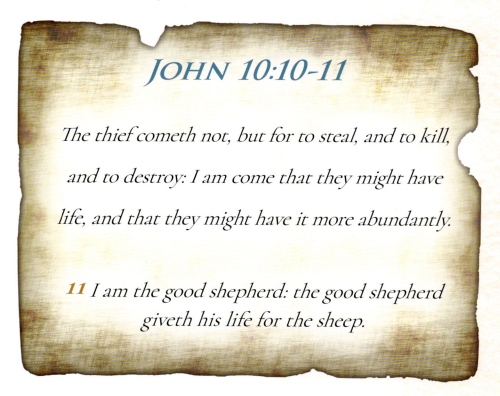

JOHN 10:10-11

The thief cometh not, but for to steal, and to kill, and to destroy: I am come that they might have life, and that they might have it more abundantly.

11 I am the good shepherd: the good shepherd giveth his life for the sheep.

CHAPTER 5

DOES JOB'S NAME MEAN ENEMY?

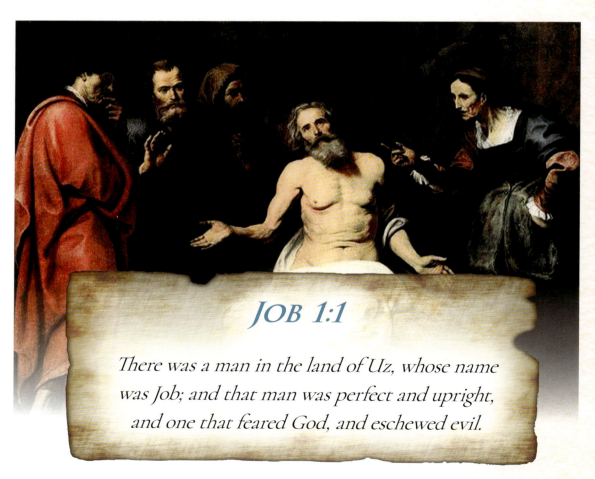

JOB 1:1

There was a man in the land of Uz, whose name was Job; and that man was perfect and upright, and one that feared God, and eschewed evil.

JOB

So, What Does JOB Mean?

We have looked at one of the most popular meanings of the name of Job, the word hate.

Now let's take a look at another popular meaning of the name of Job.

Some Bible scholars believe the name signifies one who is hated and counted as an **enemy**.

You cannot read the Biblical account without understanding that Job had an army of enemies. Job has enemies on earth and in the Heaven above the earth where Satan has temporary authority and wicked legions at his command.

The Prince of the Power of the Air and those on earth that owe allegiance to him included the Chaldeans and Sabeans who plundered Job's dwelling home and killed his servants.

These enemies were all willingly active players in the assault on righteous Job.

There was also an unseen demonic force that joined in common cause to mount an assault on Job's substance, servants and family.

The unrighteous are always eager to destroy and plunder the inheritance of the righteous.

Satan's complaint against GOD was that Job had a hedge of protection around him. That would have been a laughable statement, if not so tragic.

Of course, God has a hedge of protection around his loved ones. If God did not protect His own they would all be destroyed by Satan and his army of servants.

Are you aware that if you love the Lord then you are in a war with enemies both seen and unseen?

Ephesians 6:10-13

Finally, my brethren, be strong in the Lord, and in the power of his might. Put on the whole armour of God, that ye may be able to stand against the wiles of the devil.

For we wrestle not against flesh and blood, but against principalities, against powers, against the rulers of the darkness of this world, against spiritual wickedness in high places.

Wherefore take unto you the whole armour of God, that ye may be able to withstand in the evil day, and having done all, to stand.

The fact that many of God's children seem blissfully unaware of their Heavenly Father's constant care and protection of them is shameful and should be repented of with constant prayers of gratitude for His blessings, both seen and unseen.

Satan's complaint against God is proof positive of his single-minded arrogance and hubris.

With the hedge of protection removed, Satan would have completely destroyed Job had it not been for the commandment given by God that Job's life must be spared.

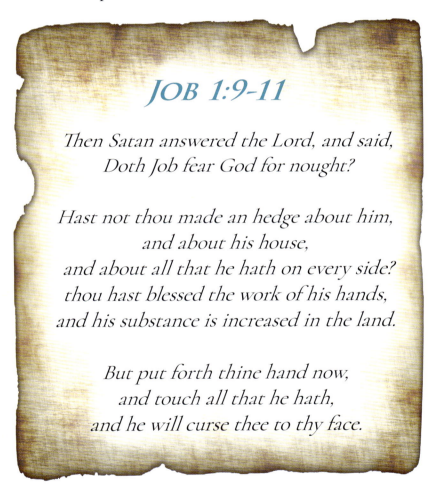

JOB 1:9-11

Then Satan answered the Lord, and said, Doth Job fear God for nought?

Hast not thou made an hedge about him, and about his house, and about all that he hath on every side? thou hast blessed the work of his hands, and his substance is increased in the land.

But put forth thine hand now, and touch all that he hath, and he will curse thee to thy face.

The reason that many Bible scholars believe that Job's name means ENEMY is because Job's name and the Hebrew word for Enemy are almost the same. Almost but not quite.

Consider the Hebrew word Job and then take a look at the Hebrew word Enemy displayed below:

Let's pause here and reflect on the Hebrew word below that is translated into English as Enemy. Notice that all the Hebrew letters in the name of **Job** are also in the Hebrew word **Enemy**.

Notice that only difference is that the Vav and the Yood are reversed.

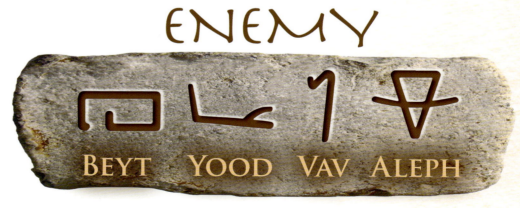

The idea of an enemy is not unfamiliar to us. An enemy is someone who seeks to damage you in some way. He may wish to appropriate your property, your wealth, or your very life.

Countries spend billions of dollars to protect its citizens from the Enemy.

Have you ever wondered what God's definition of an enemy is?

The answer can be found in the very essence of the Hebrew word we translate as Enemy.

Let's take a look at the two Picture meanings of the four-letter Hebrew word enemy.

How does God define an enemy?

Who is the ultimate enemy and what is his true purpose?

Does God have a battle plan to defeat the enemy?

The Four-Letter Hebrew Word Enemy is composed of four pictures.

ALEPH THE OX

VAV THE IRON NAIL AND WOODEN HOOK

YOOD THE HAND

BEYT THE TENT

ENEMY

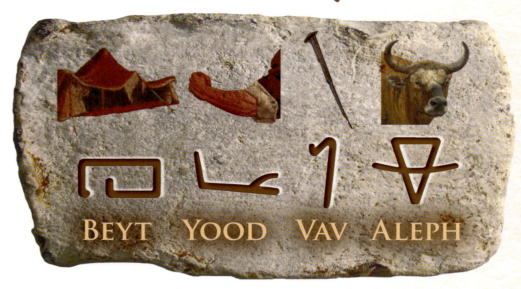

Beyt　Yood　Vav　Aleph

AUIB

Let's look at the Satanic plans of the Enemy as revealed in the Hebrew Word ENEMY.

ALEPH		The Enemy who is pictured as the Strong Leader who is the Prince of the Power of the Air.
VAV		Wants to Secure his Victory over God
YOOD		By Separating US!
BEYT		From the Household of God the Son.

JOB • The Mystery Hidden in the Hebrew Pictures and Numbers

Non-Messianic Summary Translation of Picture Narrative of the Hebrew Word Enemy.

The Strong Leader
(The Prince of the Power of the Air)
who desires to Secure a Place for us in Hell by Separating us from the Household of the Son of God.

Remember that whatever evil plans Satan has for those that love God, God has better plans. God can turn Satan's plan meant for evil into something GOOD!

This is even evident is the very words that are meant to cause us to fear and flee.

Now let's take a look at a "perfect" example of how God thwarts the plans of our arch enemy in order to accomplish something unexpected and wonderful.

However well-planned Satan's strategies for evil, God has a better more powerful plan for good.

Take a look at the MESSIANIC meaning of the Hebrew word **Enemy**.

ENEMY

AUIB

	**ALEPH** the Strong Leader who is Our Deliverer, pictured as the Prince of Heaven.
	VAV Has Secured His Victory over Satan, the Fallen Angels and all spiritual wickedness in high places by His Sacrificial death on Mount Calvary where He was nailed to a wooden cross, secured with an IRON NAIL.
	YOOD This mighty Divine Deed vanquished our Enemy Satan and all his unholy hosts.
	BEYT And secured for us a place and a position. The place is in Heaven and the position is as Sons and Daughters of the Most High God.

JOB • The Mystery Hidden in the Hebrew Pictures and Numbers

Messianic Summary Translation of Picture Narrative of the Hebrew Word Enemy.

Beyt   Yood   Vav   Aleph

God the Father is going to Re-Connect us by virtue of a Mighty Divine Deed to our Heavenly Home!

Deuteronomy 33:27

The eternal God is thy refuge, and underneath are the everlasting arms: and he shall thrust out the enemy from before thee; and shall say, Destroy them.

Choose Your Enemies Wisely!

By whatever means, Satan is driven by an insane desire to destroy any relationship between man and God.

To be a friend of God is to be by definition an enemy of Satan.

Satan knows that man was created for fellowship with God the Creator and must, according to the dictates of his withered heart, be persuaded to abandon any hope or desire for such a relationship.

The Mystery Hidden in the Hebrew Pictures and Numbers • JOB

Instead, man must be enticed to serve and worship Lucifer.

The war that encompasses the earth is multi-dimensional and multi-phased. It sometimes appears as open conflict and at other times the battle rages just under the surface where it bubbles up in repeated cycles that are each more vile and corrosive than the one before.

Underneath all the assaults against humanity by the Prince of the Power of the Air there is one unchanging foundational principle at work. It is the poisonous venom that focuses the enemy's constant barrage against all the friends of God.

Let's take a look at the Hebrew word for ENEMY to see if we might gain some insight into the reason that Satan so relished the opportunity to destroy the life of Righteous Job.

First, I would like you to carefully take a look at the four letters that compose the name of Job.

The Hebrew letters in the name JOB are *Aleph* ▽ *Yood* ∠ *Vav* ↑ *Beyt* ⊏⊐.

Now look at the four letters that compose the Hebrew word ENEMY.

The Hebrew letters in the word are *Aleph* ▽ *Vav* ↑ *Yood* ∠ *Beyt* ⊏⊐.

The Hebrew name of Job and the Hebrew name for ENEMY both contain the same letters.

Please notice that the only difference is that the *Yood* ∠ and the *Vav* ↑ are reversed.

What does this mean?

With the letters in the name of Job in mind let's see if we can discover the picture meaning of the Hebrew word ENEMY as seen in the name of JOB. The Hebrew word we translate in English as Enemy has a meaning that is tangentially connected to the name JOB as should be obvious from the similarities in the letters and pictures.

The first time we find the Hebrew word Enemy in the Scriptures is in Exodus 15:6:

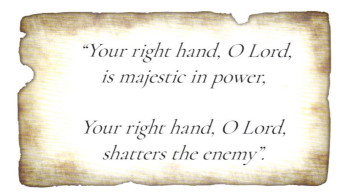

"Your right hand, O Lord, is majestic in power,

Your right hand, O Lord, shatters the enemy."

As we learned earlier in this chapter, the Hebrew word Enemy in the context of Satan has the following meaning:

THE STRONG LEADER
(The Prince of the Power of the Air)
WHO DESIRES TO SECURE A PLACE FOR US IN HELL BY SEPARATING US FROM THE HOUSEHOLD OF THE SON OF GOD.

Let's go over the meaning of Enemy **one more time** adding details and important clues as to what this is all about.

The first letter in Enemy is Aleph

THE STRONG LEADER PICTURED BY THE OX IS NOT GOD THE FATHER. OBVIOUSLY, THE STRONG LEADER IN MIND IS SATAN.

THE NUMBER ONE TELLS US THAT THIS STRONG LEADER IS THE FIRST.

The question is, the first what?

The answer is the first Rebel.

There are many illustrations in the Scripture of strong leaders.

Not all strong leaders are good.

The Kings of Israel were strong leaders and most of them were evil.

Who is it that from the beginning, our beginning on earth, has always been the enemy.

He is Lucifer the Cherub that once covered the throne of God.

He became the first creature that slandered God, and because of his rebellion was cast out of God's Heaven.

He is Satan the Accuser and Adversary of our Soul.

The Second letter in word Enemy is Vav

TO JOIN TWO THINGS TOGETHER

NUMBER OF MAN

The meaning of the Hebrew letter Vav is to attach or connect two things together.

What are those two things?

The answer is found in the two letters separated by the letter Vav ו.

The Strong Evil Leader Aleph ∀ is Connected by the letter Vav ו to the Hebrew letter Yood ⌐ pictured as doing a mighty deed or work.

YOOD
TO WORK

Pictured as a Hand

YOOD 10

ORDINAL PERFECTION

On whose behalf is this Deed being done?

What kind of Deed or Work?

We discover the answer to the first question in the number of the Hebrew letter Vav. The number SIX. Six is the number of mankind.

Is the Mighty Deed being undertaken in order to benefit mankind?

But what kind of Mighty Deed is it?

We discover the answer to that question in the fourth letter in the word ENEMY.

BEYT 2
HOUSE/HOME

The picture in view is the Home.

The letter Beyt is the number **2**. In this case, he is the one that comes along to create a division.

The picture and number meaning of ENEMY is stunning as it gets directly at the heart of the matter.

What is the Enemy attempting to do?

He is attempting to do three things at the same time.

> **1** He has come to cause division and destroy the home and all that dwell in it.

> **2** He has come to steal away our relationship with our Heavenly Father.

He has come to divide brother from brother and spoil the unity and fellowship that God desires to have with man.

In short, Satan has come to separate us from our Heavenly Home.

But there is one more thing he is trying to do.

> **3** Satan wants us to join him in his final home.

Where is that?

In Hell!

Does Satan desire our fellowship in hell?

Absolutely not!

Those who follow Satan into his final fiery abode are there to be tormented day and night. They are there as Satan's trophies of treachery to be terrorized for all eternity. Satan has convinced many fools that he is their friend.

Nothing could be further from the truth.

Satan is your enemy and if you follow him you will end up going where he goes, the Lake of Fire!

Job was not persuaded by the enemy of his soul to curse God and die.

What is the Spiritual significance of all this?

It is simply this, our home in Heaven is both blessed and eternal.

Choose your enemies wisely.

To be a friend with the world is to be an enemy of God.

> ### JAMES 4:4
> Ye adulterers and adulteresses,
> know ye not that the friendship of the world
> is enmity with God?
> whosoever therefore will be
> a friend of the world is the enemy of God.

Keep your eyes on the Lord Jesus Christ and your most blessed hopes and dreams will be realized throughout eternity.

> ### HEBREWS 12:1-2
> Wherefore seeing we also are compassed
> about with so great a cloud of witnesses,
> let us lay aside every weight,
> and the sin which doth so easily beset us,
> and let us run with patience
> the race that is set before us,
> 2 Looking unto Jesus the author
> and finisher of our faith;
> who for the joy that was set before
> him endured the cross,
> despising the shame,
> and is set down at the right hand
> of the throne of God

Finally, notice the difference between the Hebrew order of the four pictograms in the word ENEMY and compare it to the name JOB.

It is true that all the letters or symbols are the same, but the order of the Yood and Vav are reversed.

What does this mean?

The context of the name of Job is based on God's recommendation of Job as the most righteous man alive on the earth at that time.

There is a simple prophecy in the name of Job.

If you do not see it you soon will as the answer is coming up in the last chapter.

We are now beginning to uncover the clue to the real story that is hidden in the narrative regarding JOB.

CHAPTER 7

DOES JOB'S NAME MEAN GRIEVING AND GROANING?

SOME BIBLICAL SCHOLARS BELIEVE THAT THE NAME OF JOB MEANS TO GRIEVE AND TO GROAN.

Consider all the blessings that Job had received in this life as a result of his constancy and faithfulness to the LORD. Job was the wealthiest man in the land.

That all changed in a moment of time.

Job was destined, despite his love and fear for the Lord, to endure a limited but severe period of suffering and tribulation.

Hebrew names have meanings.

So, it is not unusual to imagine that the name Job contained a theological message, a spiritual virtue or a caution for good or ill.

It was not unusual for the Lord to ordain a hidden message in the names of both his servants and his enemies. As a friend of God, Job's name was designed to proclaim a message.

The question is, was it a message of grief and pain?

There is no doubt that for a very short season Job experienced a distilled and potent portion of grief.

For most of us, the experience of Job is not something we can fully understand. We have all experienced times of grief in our life, but I doubt there is anyone reading this book that has ever experienced the condensed portion of grief and suffering that was served up to God's servant Job.

I mentioned in an earlier chapter that Joseph was the shadow-type of Christ of our Savior.

I also mentioned that Job is the arch-type of those that truly love God.

But was Job more than a shadow-type of those that love God?

Let's rehearse the life of Job in order to see if we can discover a shadow of the Messiah.

 Job is presented to us as a righteous man, the most righteous man on the earth at the time. Now, to be clear, Job was clearly a sinner.

Now, consider the most righteous man to ever step foot on the earth. A man who never sinned.

What is His name?

Jesus Christ!

 At the conclusion of the story of Job, the Lord told Job's miserable comforters that He would bring a curse upon them unless Job sacrificed and interceded on their behalf.

Without the sacrifice and intercession of Jesus the Messiah we would all be under the wrath and curse of God.

3 When we first encounter Job we find him praying for his family, convinced that without God's salvation they would despise God in their hearts and perish in their sins.

Now consider our Priestly Mediator, Christ the Savior.

There is one prayer of the Lord Jesus that stands out in my mind above the rest. It was a prayer for one He loved and called a friend. His name was Simon Peter.

John 15:15

*Henceforth I call you not servants;
for the servant knoweth not what his lord doeth:
but I have called you friends;
for all things that I have heard of my Father
I have made known unto you.*

Luke 22:31-32

*And the Lord said, Simon, Simon,
behold, Satan hath desired to have you,
that he may sift you as wheat:
But I have prayed for thee,
that thy faith fail not:*

This same Jesus is now sitting at the right hand of the Father.

And what is He doing?

ROMANS 8:34

*Who is he that condemneth?
It is Christ that died, yea rather,
that is risen again,
who is even at the right hand of God,
who also maketh intercession for us.*

4 Job suffered although he was righteous and had done nothing evil.

The Lord Jesus suffered although there was no sin to be found in Him.

The difference, of course, between the suffering of Job and the suffering of Christ was the fact that Jesus knew why He was suffering and embraced it with joy in order that He might one day transport us to His Father's Kingdom.

Job did not embrace his suffering, he groaned under the weight of it and wondered why he was under, what appeared to him to be, the judgment of God.

5 In the end, Job was not only relieved of his suffering but God graciously doubled everything that Job had previously possessed and gifted him with a long and prosperous life in this world. This of course was nothing compared to the promise of life eternal in the world to come.

After His suffering, Jesus Christ returned to His home in Heaven where He is preparing a home for His beloved friends. Jesus will one day come again to this earth will He will rule and reign for a thousand years.

 The life of Job from the opening scene to the last act was a picture of God's sovereign plan to rescue those He loved in order to provide for them a Heavenly home.

If this purpose is not evident at this point in the book please keep reading as it will become clear.

Obviously, Job is only a faint shadow of the coming Messiah.

But a shadow none the less.

Good Grief!

As we mentioned earlier in this chapter there are some Bible scholars that believe the name of Job means Grief!

I can find no evidence of this in the Hebrew letters that make up the name of Job.

What I did find was a direct connection between the Messianic meaning of the name of Job and the Messianic meaning of the word Grief.

The first time the word Grief or Grieving occurs in the Bible is in Genesis 26:35.

It is no coincidence that the Hebrew word Grief is first found in connection to home and family.

So many of the pictures and numbers that are embedded in the Hebrew words are really two-sided coins, revealing both the problem and the solution.

The solution often clues you into the seriousness of the problem.

Such is the case with the Hebrew word Grief.

The manifestation of Grief is Grieving.

The first time we find the word Grieving it is meant to wake us up to what should cause us Grief.

Man's grief is often trivial and inappropriate.

The things that cause a man to grieve are a window into his soul.

Is the loss of wealth and position in this world a reason to grieve?

Men have jumped out of windows and ended their lives in a moment of grief, having lost their fortunes.

Women have committed suicide after grieving for the loss of a husband or a child.

Children grieve and cannot be comforted at the loss of a hamster or a pet dog or cat.

Adults grieve and groan when anything untoward comes into their lives.

Man's grief may seem legitimate at the time, as we all suffer loss and regret unfavorable circumstance, but is it really?

The answer is found in the Scriptures alone.

The first time the Hebrew word Grieving appears in the Bible is in Genesis 6:6.

Notice who it is that is doing the grieving. Consider the reason for the grief.

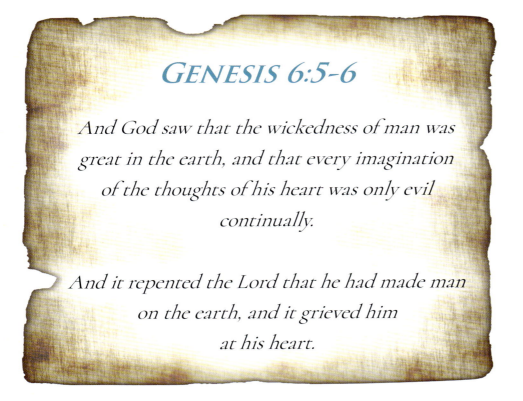

GENESIS 6:5-6

And God saw that the wickedness of man was great in the earth, and that every imagination of the thoughts of his heart was only evil continually.

And it repented the Lord that he had made man on the earth, and it grieved him at his heart.

Who is doing the grieving?

It is the Lord.

Why is the Lord grieving?

The verse answers the question.

God saw the heart of man that it was wicked and filled continually with evil imaginations continually.

Notice that there is a great gulf between what causes men and woman to grieve and what causes God to grieve.

If we look at the picture meaning for the Hebrew word Grief we are at a loss to figure out what it means.

What happens when we look at the Pictures and Numbers in the Hebrew word Grief from a Divine Perspective?

What message is being revealed?

The answer cuts to the heart of the matter as we will discover.

GRIEF

MESSIANIC MEANING OF THE THREE LETTERS IN THE HEBREW WORD GRIEF

MEM
The one letter that means water. It can be the water from a clear stream that brings life or the water from a flood or tsunami that brings death and destruction. It can also be the water that falls like the rain from the Heavens.

In the Divine context of Grief, the Mem or water that is being pictured is the water that comes down from above to bring life and nourishment to the earth and all those that dwell in it. It is a picture of the Water of Life.

REYSH
The one letter that means a head person or Prince. So, now we are to understand that the Water coming down from above is connected to an important person, a prince.

TAV
The one Hebrew pictogram that means a Covenant, a Sign and is pictured as a wooden cross.

The final clue as to the consequences, spiritual and theological meaning of Grief is revealed in the last letter, Tav ✝.

Messianic Translation of the Word Grief

The Messiah is coming down from Heaven to keep the promise made to our first parents, Adam and Eve. He is coming down to cancel the covenant that Adam made with death and hell.

HE IS COMING DOWN TO FULFILL THE SIGN OF THAT COVENANT AS PLANNED IN HEAVEN BY HIS FATHER. HE IS COMING TO WILLINGLY GIVE UP HIS LIFE ON A WOODEN CROSS IN ORDER TO ASSUAGE THE FATHER'S GRIEF WITH SINFUL MAN AND FORGE A PATH OF PEACE BETWEEN GOD AND MAN BY THE SHEDDING OF HIS OWN BLOOD ON THE CROSS OF CALVARY.

When you consider the first mention of grieving, consider that it was the condition of the heart of man that caused our Heavenly Father to grieve. Consider also that it was the knowledge that only the sacrifice of His Son could remedy this seemingly hopeless condition that would be the remedy. This was a grievous condition indeed!

All of this was in our Heavenly Father's heart when He grieved.

It was a noble grief that both punishes and preserves.

Everything with God is good, even Grief!

Consider the consequences of God's Grief and reflect on its goodness.

Isaiah 53:3-5

He is despised and rejected of men;
a man of sorrows, and acquainted with **grief:**
and we hid as it were our faces from him;
he was despised,
and we esteemed him not.

Surely, he hath borne our **griefs,**
and carried our sorrows:
yet we did esteem him stricken,
smitten of God, and afflicted.

But he was wounded for our transgressions,
he was bruised for our iniquities:
the chastisement of our peace was upon him;
and with his stripes we are healed.

CHAPTER 8

THE MEANING OF JOB'S NAME

JOB 3:3
*Let the day perish wherein I was born,
and the night in which it was said,
There is a man child conceived.*

here are still others that believe the name of Job was an expression of the love and desire that his parents experienced when Job was born.

We can read the opposite sentiment in the lamentations of Job found in Job 3:3. Job expressed the sincere desire that he had never been born. If there is a message of love and deep desire for the welfare of Job hidden in his name it would not be strange to hear the bearer of that name regret his own birth during a time of deep sorrow.

What does JOB mean?

As we discovered in the previous chapter, some believe the name JOB signifies one who is hated and counted as an enemy.

Many Hebrew language scholars disagree and believe the name of Job was an expression of the love and desire that his parents experienced when Job was born.

We have already explored the Hebrew word for enemy as a possible meaning in our last chapter.

Let's examine the Picture meaning of Love as we ask the question:

What does Job mean?

Let's review the name Job as we examine the four-letter Hebrew word JOB spelled Aleph, Yood, Vav and Beyt.

Can you remember what we discovered when we put the pictures and the number together?

⊽	**ALEPH**	The Strong Leader
⌐	**YOOD**	Hand doing a work
۱	**VAV**	Fastened Together
⊐	**BEYT**	A House or a Tent

JOB • The Mystery Hidden in the Hebrew Pictures and Numbers

Now let's take a look at the Hebrew word for Love.

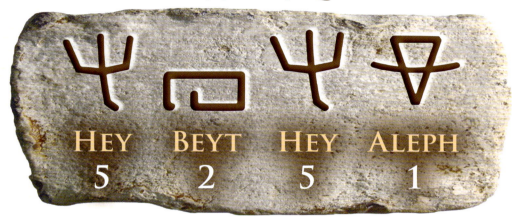

LOVE

Hey	Beyt	Hey	Aleph
5	2	5	1

AHAVAH

Now let's take a look at the Hebrew word for Love.

	ALEPH	Strong Leader – First – God the Father	OX
	HEY	Reveal – Look – Holy Spirit	BEHOLD
	BEYT	House – Tent – Son – Family Son of God	TENT / HOUSE
	HEY	Reveal – Look – Holy Spirit	BEHOLD

There are two possible Picture meanings of the Hebrew word Love. The one that is the most likely translation is as follows:

GOD THE FATHER REVEALS HIMSELF TO US THROUGH HIS ONLY BEGOTTEN SON.

The Mystery Hidden in the Hebrew Pictures and Numbers • JOB

John 1:18

*No man hath seen God at any time, the only begotten Son, which is in the bosom of the **Father**, he hath declared him.*

John 5:20

For the Father loveth the Son, and sheweth him all things that himself doeth: and he will shew him greater works than these, that ye may marvel.

Now we are going to explore the Numeric Meaning of LOVE and how it relates to the Messianic Message embedded in the name of JOB.

NUMERIC

LOVE

| Hey | Beyt | Hey | Aleph |
| 5 | 2 | 5 | 1 |

The numbers in the Hebrew word LOVE are:

1	ALEPH	Diety – Unity – Sufficiency Independence – The First One is Indivisible	GOD THE FATHER
5	HEY	Unmerited Favor God's Goodness Pentateuch Divine Strength - The Fifth	GRACE
2	BEYT	Difference – Good or Evil Division – Living Word Second To Come Alongside for Help	GOD THE SON
5	HEY	Unmerited Favor God's Goodness Pentateuch Divine Strength - The Fifth	GRACE

The obvious Number meaning is easy to understand, it is the abundance of GRACE freely ordained by the Father and GRACE freely offered by the SON OF GOD.

If you combine the Picture and Number meaning of LOVE, what do you get?

BEHOLD THE GRACIOUS PLANS OF THE FATHER
BEHOLD THE GRACIOUS DIVINE DEED OF THE SON

Love is not an idea, it is a Person. God is Love!

How is this Love Expressed?

How did God LOVE the World?

The answer is not found in the sentimental meaning, a wishful thinking of LOVE.

Most Christians would answer this question by turning to and reading John 3:16:

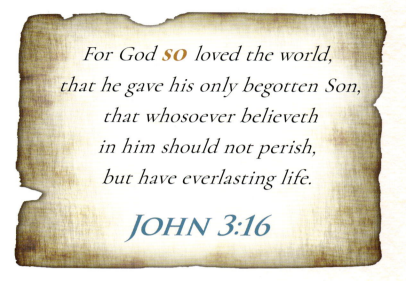

For God **so** loved the world, that he gave his only begotten Son, that whosoever believeth in him should not perish, but have everlasting life.

JOHN 3:16

If you ask 1000 Christians what this verse means, 999 will give you the wrong answer.

The overwhelming majority of Christians have memorized this verse and if you ask them to share its meaning they will confidently tell you that this verse is about **how much God loves** the world and the provision He made in His only begotten Son in order that believers should not perish.

Sounds pretty New Testament!

Right?

Actually, the truth that Jesus disclosed to Nicodemus that night in Jerusalem was the very clue that unlocks the mystery of the promise that God made to Adam and Eve almost 4000 years earlier.

And just so you wouldn't miss it, the Holy Spirit arranged it so the first promise of Redemption is made in Genesis 3:15.

Genesis is the first book of the Old Testament that begins with these words, "In the beginning God."

And where did the Holy Spirit arrange for you to find the answer to the Messianic mystery and hope that had filled every God-fearing person who ever walked the earth?

Look where the Holy Spirit arranged that this puzzle piece might be found.

It is found in John 3:16, the only book in the New Testament that begins with, "In the beginning was the WORD."

And who does John tell us the WORD is?

The WORD is God.

Let's look at that promise found in Genesis 3:15.

And I will put enmity between thee and the woman, and between thy seed and her seed; it shall bruise thy head, and thou shalt bruise his heel.

God does everything very precisely.

Is there a pattern laid over on itself in the match up Genesis 3:15 and John 3:16?

If the prophecy found in Genesis 3:15 is a prophecy about the redemption found in the death of Yeshua Ha-Mashiach, Jesus the Christ, then it should conform to the most prominent disclosure of that truth found in the New Testament.

Let's look at the disclosure in the Gospel of John and see if we can find the scarlet thread of truth that closes this circle.

Words matter,
Big ones and little ones!

Words are important and they mean something!

This is the notation I keep sending to myself as a reminder of how important it is to actually understand what God is revealing.

The key to unlocking the real meaning of John 3:16 is found in one small little overlooked and misunderstood word.

The word is "SO."

The Living Bible paraphrases the verse in a way that is consistent with most people's understanding of the message found in John 3:16.

LIVING BIBLE - For God loved the world **so much** that he gave his only Son so that anyone who believes in him shall not perish but have eternal life.

Notice the emphasis.

According to the Living Bible, what is being revealed?

The answer is **HOW MUCH** God loved the world.

But is this what Jesus actually said?

Unfortunately, our common understanding of the KJV translation of John 3:16 is based on a 21st century understanding of the word SO that is completely out of harmony and inconsistent with the usage of the word SO in 1611, the year the KJV was translated into English.

A quick reference to a Greek New Testament will immediately inform you that the word translated "SO" doesn't mean "SO MUCH."

The word translated "SO" is the Greek word οὕτως or outos.

Outos means, "In this way" or "this is the way."

What is the Apostle John trying to communicate to the reader?

Is he communicating HOW MUCH God loved the world?

The answer is an emphatic NO.

God is communicating the WAY IN WHICH God loved the world.

When this was translated into the English KJV it was translated correctly since the understanding of the word "SO" in 1611 England meant "Like So," not "So Much."

The Greek word outos shows up hundreds of times in the New Testament.

If you take a look at the introduction to the Lord's Prayer, you will see that "outos" is translated "After this manner" in the KJV.

This figure of speech is Old English but has the correct meaning to this day.

Other English translations use variations of the same concept.

The Greek word "Outos" is translated "like this" and "this is how."

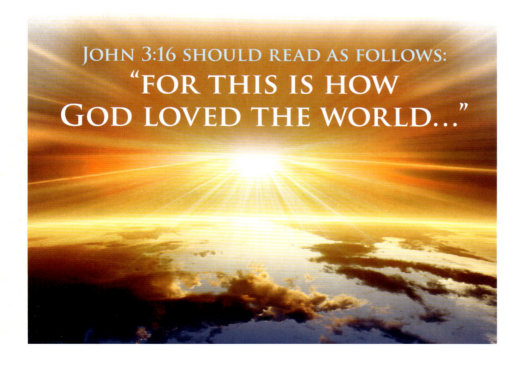

JOHN 3:16 SHOULD READ AS FOLLOWS:
"FOR THIS IS HOW GOD LOVED THE WORLD…"

The obvious question is HOW?

How did God Love the World?

The translators of the KJV knew what the Greek word "outos" meant and translated it correctly based on how the word was commonly used in the 17th century.

Modern Bible translators also know what the word means and instead of re-translating it so that modern English readers understand what God is saying through his servant John they make a deep bow to the traditions of men and ignore the true meaning.

If you doubt this, simply take a look at the margin notes next to John 3:16 in the ESV translation and you will see that they have a footnote that correctly exegetes the Scripture and yet are bound by tradition to translate it in a way certain to be misunderstood by the modern English reader.

Now back to John 3:16

In order to understand what is being communicated by the Apostle John, we need to widen the lens in order to comprehend what John had in view when he made the statement, "this is the way that God loved the world."

Let's ask the question that Jesus expected those that read His revelation to ask.

In what way did God love the world?

John 3:16 is not about how much God loved the world but the way in which he loved the world.

What is that way?

Is there a problem with reading John 3:16 by itself?

The answer is YES!

How many sermons have we heard about how much God loves the world using John 3:16 as a proof text?

Make no mistake about it, God does love the world.

The problem is that John 3:16 is not about how much God loved the world, it is about something even more incredible.

It is about HOW God loved the world!

Let's let Jesus solve this misunderstanding for us.

Look at John 3:16 in the context of what Jesus revealed to Nicodemus.

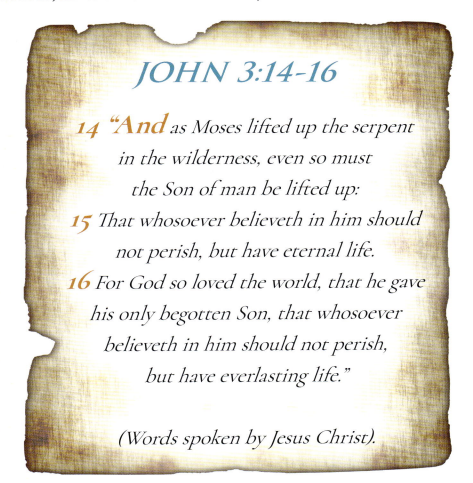

JOHN 3:14-16

14 "**And** as Moses lifted up the serpent in the wilderness, even so must the Son of man be lifted up:
15 That whosoever believeth in him should not perish, but have eternal life.
16 For God so loved the world, that he gave his only begotten Son, that whosoever believeth in him should not perish, but have everlasting life."

(Words spoken by Jesus Christ).

All of a sudden, John 3:16 means something completely different than we originally thought.

But what exactly is this all about?

In order to discover the true meaning and its connection to the prophecy proclaimed in Genesis 3:15, we need to do a little more homework.

The significance of the "brazen serpent" that Moses lifted up in the wilderness is not explained anywhere in Scripture until we find its meaning disclosed by Yeshua Ha-Mashiach, Jesus the Christ.

The story surrounding the brazen serpent is told in detail and it would profit us greatly to read and understand it.

The record of the brazen serpent is found in Numbers 21:4-8.

4 From Mount Hor they set out by the way to the Red Sea, to go around the land of Edom. And the people became impatient on the way. 5 And the people spoke against God and against Moses, "Why have you brought us up out of Egypt to die in the wilderness? For there is no food and no water, and we loathe this worthless food." 6 Then the Lord sent fiery serpents among the people, and they bit the people, so that many people of Israel died. 7 And the people came to Moses and said, "We have sinned, for we have spoken against the Lord and against you. Pray to the Lord, that he take away the serpents from us." So Moses prayed for the people. 8 And the Lord said to Moses, "Make a fiery serpent and set it on a pole, and everyone who is bitten, when he sees it, shall live."

Does this dramatic case of physical salvation in the Old Testament illustrate spiritual salvation in the New Testament?

How startling!

In the midst of the seething, writhing, shrieking mass of humanity there rises a lonely pole.

In the midst of a vast hoard of human sinners, sin-bitten, dying…there rises a lonely cross!

It was our Lord who said that just as the uplifted serpent was the only means of deliverance then, so the uplifted Son of Man is the only means of deliverance now.

Can you imagine the terror that must have gripped the man or woman bitten by one of the flying fiery serpents?

All one had to do was look around and see the stricken dead bodies of those who had already succumbed to the bitter venomous poison of the serpent.

The ancient prophetic text informs us "many people of Israel died."

There is an old saying that nothing heightens the senses and focuses the mind like the gallows being built outside your prison window the night before your hanging.

This is a good illustration considering the stinging bite and excruciating pain that followed the course of the poison as it invaded every part of the victim's senses.

But, is there not an even more urgent picture of the state of mind required to be one of the "Despairing?"

Our Lord directs us to view through the lens of sacred text the true condition of men who have the venom of the serpent coursing through our veins.

Were these the ones Jesus came to save?

Is the Savior's death the means by which sinful man will once again find true comfort and rest?

The simple answer to this question has been purposely scrambled in order to make it puzzling.

The Universalist would tell us that God is obligated to save all mankind, as anything else is a betrayal of His loving nature.

Is this right?

The Scriptures do not reveal a universal salvation.

In picture and in type the Lord Jesus reveals to Nicodemus that there is a condition put upon man in order that he might be delivered. This condition as illustrated in the story of the brazen serpent is that God will not lay aside His holiness and justice in order that He might wink at sin without some extreme remedial act.

A PRICE MUST BE PAID!

Jesus stood in front of Nicodemus and declared to him in a picture that could not be ignored that He was the Price to be paid. He was the Ransom paid. It was His blood, the Perfect and Spotless Son of God, that was required as the payment for man's sin.

I promised you at the beginning of this section of John 3:16 that I would show you how the message found in John 3:14-16 is a fulfillment of a prophetic pattern laid out for us in the first promise God made to fallen man.

Genesis 3:15 is the first promise or unconditional covenant that YHVH (the LORD) made with man as recorded in the original conventional Hebrew scriptures.

This promise was the touchstone for all the promises that followed. It was on the basis of this verse that our first parents looked for the coming Redeemer.

God is very precise! Look at Genesis 3:14-15 as a pattern that is perfectly laid over on itself in John 3:14-15.

Genesis 3:14-15

14 And the Lord God said unto the **serpent,** Because thou hast done this, thou art **cursed** above all cattle, and above every beast of the field; upon thy belly shalt thou go, and dust shalt thou eat all the days of thy life:

15 And I will put enmity between thee and the woman, and between thy seed and her seed; it shall bruise thy head, and thou shalt bruise his heel.

John 3:14-15

14 And as Moses lifted up the serpent in the wilderness, even so must the Son of man be lifted up:

15 That whosoever believeth in him should not perish, but have eternal life.

Pattern is Prophecy!

For those of you that may still be having a little difficulty connecting the dots, let me see if I can be of some assistance. Think about the following bullet points and see how it threads the two passages separated by 4000 years of history together in a seamless prophetic tapestry.

Notice the Serpent in both Genesis 3:14 and John 3:14.

Notice that the Serpent in Genesis 3:14 is being cast down and cursed.

Notice that the Serpent in John 3:14 is being lifted up.

Notice that the Serpent in Genesis 3:15 causes Enmity and Separation.

Notice that the Serpent in John 3:15 Rescues and Restores.

Notice that believing the Serpent in Genesis 3:15 brought the curse of sin and death upon all mankind.

Notice that the Son of God was pointing Nicodemus to the "brass serpent" Moses lifted up in the wilderness.

This narrative from the Old Testament had a meaning that had never been revealed until Jesus revealed it to Nicodemus.

The brazen Serpent was a shadow-type of the redemptive work He was about to do on the cross. Looking to the Son of God, just as looking at the brass serpent so many years ago, would bring life.

What kind of life?
Eternal Life!

What does this have to do with the meaning of the name of JOB?

The answer is simple.

Job's name is a prophetic Harbinger that promises that in the end Job is going to end up in the household of his Heavenly Father. In other words, Job is promised Eternal Life!

Job himself prophesied how this was going to happen and we can read it in Job 19:25-27:

> For I know that my redeemer liveth,
> and that he shall stand at the latter day upon the earth:
>
> And though after my skin worms destroy this body,
> yet in my flesh shall I see God:
>
> Whom I shall see for myself,
> and mine eyes shall behold, and not another;
> though my reins be consumed within me.

The question is this: Were the promises made to Job and the promises made to Nicodemus thousands of years later the same promises?

Is there a crimson scarlet thread that weaves its way through the entire Bible from the book of Job to Gospel of John?

The answer is found in the Picture and Number meaning in the name of Job. A name we are unfolding one page at a time.

The final pages will disclose both a mystery and a promise that is hidden in the name of Job just as it was hidden in the narrative of the brazen serpent.

These two stories may not seem to be connected, but they are in ways you could never have imagined.

Please keep reading.

Now let's look at the Numeric meaning and translation of the Hebrew word LOVE.

Numeric Translation of Love
Theological and Prophetic

ALEPH 1
GOD THE FATHER

HEY 5
GRACE

BEYT 2
GOD THE SON

HEY 5
GRACE

Summary of Numeric Translation

The Love of God the Father is revealed through God the Son.

The Son of God's love for His Father is expressed in the incarnation and finally in the Redemptive work that He did on the Cross of Calvary.

God loved us through the obedience of His Son.

Luke 10:22

All things are delivered to me of my Father: and no man knoweth who the Son is, but the Father; and who the Father is, but the Son, and he to whom the Son will reveal him.

We have experienced the Amazing Grace of God because the Son of God obeyed God the Father with joy in order that we might be redeemed and re-united in fellowship with our Heavenly Father.

JOHN 14:9

*Jesus saith unto him, Have I been so long time with you, and yet hast thou not known **me** Philip? he that hath **seen me** hath **seen** the Father; and how sayest thou then, Show us the Father?*

IS THE MESSAGE OF LOVE AND DESIRE HIDDEN IN THE NAME OF JOB?

If you explore the word **DESIRE** in your English Bible and then search out the reference in Hebrew you will soon discover that the English word desire is not always translated very precisely.

The English word **Desire** could be supported by several Hebrew words that literally should be translated as anything from yearning to seeking, lusting after to coveting.

The sentiment that was most likely in the minds of the parents of Job would not have included any of the above.

There is really only one Hebrew word that fully discloses what must have been in the minds of Job's mother and father.

Love and **Desire**.

Perhaps the naming of JOB expressed by the parent of Job is disclosed in the concept of yearning and supported by the following four-letter Hebrew word spelled Tav, Aleph, Vav and Hey.

We will now take a look at the Hebrew word we translate into English as Desire!

DESIRE

HEY	VAV	ALEPH	TAV
5	6	1	400

The first time we find the English word Desire or Desired is in Genesis 3:6.

> And when the woman saw
> that the tree was good for food,
> and that it was pleasant to the eyes,
> and a tree to be **desired** to make one wise,
> she took of the fruit thereof, and did eat,
> and gave also unto her husband with her;
> and he did eat.

The literal meaning of the Hebrew word Tav ✝ Aleph ⴲ Vav ⴶ Hey ⴲ as first found in Genesis 3:6 is to **yearn** for or **yearning**.

If Job's parents named him with the thought of expressing love and desire in the very letters of his name, then Job himself seems to have undone the sentiment as we discover in Job 3:3 where Job says the following:

> *Let the day perish wherein I was born,*
> *and the night in which it was said,*
> *There is a man child conceived.*

If there is a message of deep desire for the welfare of Job hidden in his name would it not be strange to hear the bearer of that name desire that he had ever been born?

Job literally regrets his own birth.

Desire can be a fickle and uncertain thing.

Consider Eve whose desire was for wisdom and immortality.

Are these desires evil?

Of course not.

The first clue as to the secret mystery of DESIRE is hidden in the first two letters of the Hebrew word DESIRE.

There is a Desire that is Good and Healthy.

A Desire that results in light and life.

There is also a desire that may appear to be good and healthy and yet it produces Confusion, Destruction and Death.

How can you tell the difference?

Notice the first two letters in the Hebrew word Desire.

DESIRE

Hey	Vav	Aleph	Tav
5	6	1	400

We know that Aleph  and Tav are the first and the last letters of the Hebrew Aleph-Beyt. In English, we might say A to Z. In Greek, we would say the Alpha and the Omega.

Tav   Aleph

114

There are two big ideas contained in the **Aleph** ⅁ and the **Tav** ✝.

Remember that **Aleph** ⅁ is the first letter in the Hebrew Aleph-Beyt and **Tav** ✝ is the last letter.

The Beginning and the End, the Entire Word of God, the Alpha and the Omega are ALL expressed by the first and last letters of the Aleph-Beyt.

Both these big ideas have one personage in mind.

That person is known as the Alpha and the Omega and the Living Word. His name is Yeshua Ha-Mashiach, Jesus the Christ.

All Godly Desire can only begin with the Aleph ⅁ and the Tav ✝.

What happens when you reverse the Aleph ⅁ and the Tav ✝, when you pervert God the creator's hierarchal order of things creating confusion where clarity once existed?

What happens when you call Good Evil and Evil Good?

The first two letters in the Hebrew word Desire alert us to the fact that something is not right, something is backward and confused.

Something has been turned on its head.

Since the fall of Adam, all of man's desires have been tainted with sin and rebellion.

Even our best desires are not without the leaven of unrighteousness, impure motives and sin.

The Tav ✝ followed by the Aleph ∀ sends a clear message that something is amiss.

The next letter in the Hebrew Word we translate into English as Desire creates a transition. It tells us that we are looking at one thing that is attached to another thing.

The third letter in the Hebrew word Desire is the Vav .

Vav is pictured as an IRON NAIL. It tells us that two concepts are being joined together.

So, the question is; what two things are being joined together by the Iron Nail?

The answer is found in the fourth letter in the Hebrew word we translate as DESIRE.

The Hebrew letter HEY is the picture of Revelation. While this picture often refers to the Holy Spirit, we must wonder out loud if that is the picture God had in mind.

If the Tav and the Aleph were reversed it would be simple to translate DESIRE as the Aleph and the Tav, the Beginning and the End, the Son of God secured by Revelation from the Holy Spirit.

The problem is that we are not looking at the Aleph and the Tav, we are looking at the reversal of the Tav and the Aleph, a reversal of the Aleph and the Tav.

What does this mean?

The reversal of the Aleph and the Tav tells us that our desires have been perverted. We are no longer listening to the true word of God but a substitute, a perversion of the word.

Something false is being revealed.

When you look at the scene in the Garden of Eden, you can easily understand that the Desire that lit up in the heart and mind of Eve was not the result of a true revelation from God.

It was rather a perversion and challenge to the Aleph and the Tav, the entirety of God's revelatory word.

The first time the word Desire or Desired show up in Scripture is in Genesis 3:6. Read what it says.

GENESIS 3:6

*And when the woman saw
that the tree was good for food,
and that it was pleasant to the eyes,
and a tree to be **desired** to makeone wise,
she took of the fruit thereof,
and did eat,
and gave also unto her husband with her;
and he did eat.*

To be clear, the word Desired and Desire are both the same.

DESIRED

HEY	VAV	ALEPH	TAV
5	6	1	400

The big question in life is simply this:

Who are you going to listen to?
Who is the voice of authority in your life?
What do you desire more than anything else?

If you think there is nothing hopeful in the four-letter Hebrew word Desire let me assure that there is.

There is both a challenge and a promise in the picture and number message of the Hebrew word Desire and Desired. Let's take a look.

Tav is pictured as crossed sticks and it means a sign or a covenant.

Tav is also the number 400, a number that is the multiplication of 10 (Ordinal Perfection) and 40 (Creation and Probation).

There is a promise in the number 400, an undeserved grace that comes unexpectantly at the end of man's probationary period on the earth. A probation that man has failed miserably and yet man's failure does not end in the way you would expect.

Instead, there is Revival and Renewal as a result of God's mercy and grace.

Tav ✝ as the first letter in the Hebrew word desire informs us that man has made a covenant with death and hell.

Tav ✝ pictures a cross, an instrument of punishment and death. This death is by all rights the birthright of fallen man who has listened to the voice of Satan and plunged the world into chaos, confusion and death.

The Cross that man deserves is supernaturally borne by the Son of God who nullifies the covenant that man has made with Death by offering up Himself as the sacrifice for man's sin.

God secures Man to the Revelation of Everlasting Life.

The Supernatural meaning of Desire points us to the finished work of the Cross of Calvary. Man has turned God's revelation on its head resulting in a sinful rebellion that deserved nothing short of death. God in His love and great mercy took the perversion and turned it into Salvation. What man deserved would be borne by God's Son on a cross in order that we might once again be at peace and in harmony with our Creator. This has all been made possible because of God's DESIRE to reconcile man to Himself through the majestic accomplishment of His only begotten Son who was lifted up on a Cross as a symbol of the Curse of Sin, just like the brazen serpent, in order that we might look and live.

CHAPTER 9

HIDDEN MEANING REVEALED IN THE NAME OF JOB!

Is there ANOTHER Hidden Message in the Name of JOB?

It is only when we consider the Scriptures as it gives a full account from beginning to end of the story of Job that we are fully able to understand the mysteries hidden in Job's name.

The mystery of the message we are meant to discover in the name of Job is hidden in the pictures and numbers of his name and can only be understood as they are overlaid on the biblical narrative.

The pictures and numbers revealed in the Hebrew letters are not separate revelations; they are there to amplify and magnify the conventional text.

They are not secrets; they are witnesses to the truth of Scripture.

Does Job mean Enemy?

Does Job mean Grieving and Groaning?

Does Job mean Love and Desire?

It is not a coincidence that the message in the pictures and numbers hint at all three of the conjectures made by Biblical scholars regarding the name of Job.

If you trace out the meaning of Job based on the conventional root Hebrew word for Job all three of those meanings are both possible and present.

If that was all that was revealed then we could stop our study of the meaning of the name of Job and simply reduce it to a one-sentence summary.

We might just say that the disclosure in the name of Job is about the hatred of a malicious enemy. As a consequence, Job is groaning and grieving under the heavy weight of the loss of his possessions and his family.

You might conclude that the story of Job is about the final victory over all his enemies both seen and unseen. It is about the constancy of love for God through the trials that refine and reveal patience.

This is a popular summary of the life of Job.

We can see the patience of Job in his constancy and unwavering confidence in God.

We can feel his pain and sorrow.

We can rejoice in Job's final victory and be encouraged by his reward.

Is this what the name of Job is all about?

The answer is NO!

I can assure you that while this summary contains many kernels of truth, it is flawed.

The above summary does include some of the subplots of the story of Job but it completely misses the tapestry of truth revealed in the name and life of Job. It misses the BIG PICTURE.

The book of Job and the revelation hidden in his name is not primarily about the patience and endurance of Job.

It is not about his suffering and pain.

It is not about his overcoming.

Before we reveal the true picture and number meaning of JOB, let's look at one final clue that is hidden in his name. A clue that points us in the direction of the Big and important Picture hidden in plain sight in the name of Job.

In order to accomplish this, we need to look again and carefully at the pictures connected to each of the four letters in the name of JOB.

But it does point you in that direction.

So, in order that you understand the true meaning of the name of the man that was caught up in a drama in which he was both a participant and a prize, a player and a pawn, let's investigate the idea that Job means Hated or Enemy.

As we look at the name of Job, the first thing that I notice is the first two letters and the first two pictures of the Ox and the Hand.

In order to help us understand the picture, we will display the Hand or Yood that is separating one thing from another.

BEYT   YOOD   ALEPH

Did you know that Aleph Yood is a Hebrew word all by itself? God often nests words inside words in order to help us dig out the meaning of His revelation.

YOOD   ALEPH

The first two letters in Job's four-letter name compose the Hebrew word we translate into English as **"Where?"**

A picture really is worth a thousand words and the Picture of the Strong Leader putting his hand up in order to prevent us from seeing something is the perfect picture of WHERE.

Where is it?

I can't see it.

It is hidden behind the hand that is covering it up.

Are you starting to get the picture?

WHERE?

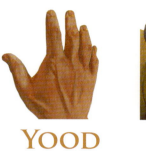 

YOOD   ALEPH

Aleph Yood can be understood as the Hand of the Strong leader that causes a separation. This is exactly what is revealed in the name Elohim.

ELOHIM

MEM   YOOD   HEY   LAMED   ALEPH

Notice the picture of the letter Yood, the Hand separating the waters from the waters.

Aleph Yood () is the Hebrew word "WHERE?"

Do you see the pictures of the hand that causes a separation between Aleph (the picture of the Father) and something else?

In order to find out what the "something else" is requires the addition of another letter.

A number of letters can be used creating many Hebrew words based on adding a letter to the Aleph and the Yood.

CALAMITY

DALET   YOOD   ALEPH

For example, the word Calamity is the Hebrew word Aleph Yood, the first two letters in the name of Job with the added Dalet.

The picture meaning is "Where is the Doorway?"

The ideal Doorway in mind is the doorway that leads to eternal life.

Let's review the meaning of the Hebrew Word Calamity.

The picture meaning displays the hand of God blocking those who are in deliberate and rebellious unbelief from finding the True Door and the Eternal Pathway it guards.

The consequence of Unbelief is Spiritual Blindness.

The consequence is Calamity.

The sad cry of the Picture meaning of Calamity is:

WHERE IS THE PATHWAY THAT LEADS TO ETERNAL LIFE?

ANGER

Now let's take a look at another example of how the Aleph and Yood, the Hebrew word for "WHERE?" is used.

First, Second and Fourth Letters in Name of JOB
Remember the Hebrew reads from Right to Left

In the case of the first, second and fourth letter in the name of Job, we see a picture of the Father separated from the Son.

Where is the Father?

Remove the letter Vav (the letter that is translated as the conjunction "and") from the name of Job and we are left with the question, "Where is the Father?" the Hebrew word we translate as ANGER.

Picture Meaning

"Where is the Father?"

The entire goal of Satan was to remove the connection between Job and his Heavenly Father. Make no mistake; Satan was doing his best to destroy that bond.

The Prince of Darkness was sure that once that connection was removed that Job would be filled with anger and bitterness. Satan was sure that any desire to worship God would wither and die.

Satan was doing all he could to induce Job to curse God.

How many people have we known who have at their disposal the complete revelation of God from Genesis to Revelation? Consider Job, living at a time when there was no written revelation. Consider those to whom much spiritual light has been given who end up spiritually shipwrecked as a result of a trial that is tiny in comparison to what Job experienced. When trials come, there are many whose faith and confidence in God is almost instantly dissolved by cruel circumstances.

This lack of confidence can be triggered by the untimely death of a child, or the unwelcome arrival of an unexpected medical condition.

What happens when a little pain and suffering intrudes into some "Christian's" lives? Many, not all, end up blaming God for their problems as their faith and confidence in His promise are thrown overboard.

What is left?

What is left is the smoldering coals of anger that burns like a fever whose heat ignites the poisonous fumes of hatred and bitterness.

Who is that anger usually directed at?

Is it directed at Satan, the evil adversary who is a murderer and a liar?

We all know that only rarely is the actual culprit held accountable.

Consider that this life and the misery, death and poverty that attends it all had its beginning before Adam was ever created.

The epicenter of all evil began with Lucifer and his prideful rebellion against the God that created him with privileges never before given to a creature.

Is the fallen Cherub Lucifer the target of man's complaints?

Does the Prince of Darkness who was the progenitor of every evil device known to man and all the sorrowful consequences that follow "called out" to stand up and admit his crime?

Sadly, the answer is NO!

In most cases, the poisonous darts of insinuation and slander are almost always directed at God.

Satan is the one that delights in the trials and sorrows of man, while God delights in mankind's eternal prosperity.

The great deceiver takes careful pains to make sure that God is falsely accused for his treachery.

Much of the burning anger results in a battle cry of rebellion that is rooted in the anguished cry "WHERE IS THE FATHER?"

Where was God when I really needed Him?

Why did He allow this to happen to me?

This was the response that Satan was sure would soon be springing from what he imagined would be the bitter and broken heart of Job.

Satan in the particular case of Job was miffed and disappointed.

Instead of an emotional outburst against God, Job remained constant and steady in his faith and confidence in the Lord through the multitude of misery he both witnessed and experienced.

Surely Job would curse God when the physical afflictions began.

Satan certainly thought he would.

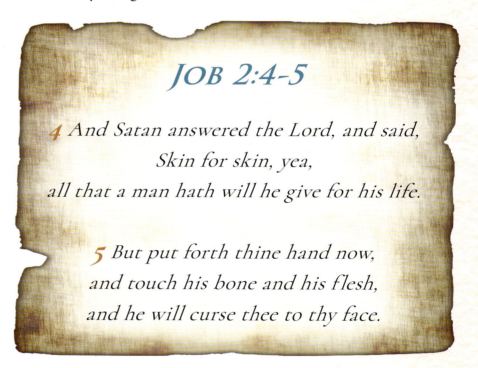

JOB 2:4-5

4 And Satan answered the Lord, and said,
Skin for skin, yea,
all that a man hath will he give for his life.

5 But put forth thine hand now,
and touch his bone and his flesh,
and he will curse thee to thy face.

Satan was absolutely sure that when physical torment was added to the emotional anguish it would seal his triumph and reveal God's misplaced commendation of Job.

But instead, it is faithfully recorded for our own instruction exactly what Job did in the face of all the calamities that fell upon him.

In Job chapter 1:20-22 we read:

> Then Job arose, and rent his mantle,
> and shaved his head,
> and fell down upon the ground,
> and worshipped, And said,
> Naked came I out of my mother's womb,
> and naked shall I return thither:
> the Lord gave, and the Lord hath taken away;
> blessed be the name of the Lord.
> In all this Job sinned not,
> nor charged God foolishly.

In the end, Satan was forced to finally admit that Job was not a hypocrite.

Job did not worship God as a means to obtaining a prosperous life.

Job's trust in God did not disappear when his wealth and family were destroyed.

God, who sees the heart, knew that Job truly loved and feared Him.

Job was not perfect but Job was just as good as God said he was.

Job was as good as he seemed to be.

CHAPTER 10
JOB'S MISERABLE COMFORTERS

It is wonderful to have friends, but with friends like Job's, who needs enemies?

In order to understand the 29 chapters that are filled with the pious and long-winded admonitions from Job's three friends, we need to understand who it is that is provoking this drama.

Did God send these friends to "comfort" Job in his time of suffering?

The answer is NO.

Satan sent them, and they must be viewed in the same light as the Sabeans, Chaldeans, wind and fire that Satan had used to bring Job to the point of abject poverty of both body and soul.

When we examine the "comforting words" of Eliphaz, Bildad, and Zophar we discover that all their high-sounding platitudes regarding God are based on their own experience, history or human experience and baseless assumptions that are groundless and irrelevant.

In a word, they are false accusations.

For 29 chapters we are treated to religious high-sounding slander that is straight from the corrupted mind of man and the pit of hell. Satan is the root of these false accusations that are based on half-truths and baseless assumptions regarding Job and God.

Is it any wonder that in the end these faithless friends are told that except Job prayerfully meditate and offer sacrifices on their behalf that they will be judged and cursed by God Himself?

Let's examine the Hebrew word for COMFORT.

HE SHALL COMFORT

"THIS SAME SHALL COMFORT US."

The first time the word comfort appears in Scripture is in the 5th chapter of Genesis.

Noah, the 10th Patriarch in the line of Adam, is named by his father Lamech.

The name Noah is spelled Noon ⁓ Chet ⊓.

We are told that Noah found grace in the eyes of the Lord and so it should be no surprise that his name contains the same two letters as the Hebrew word for Grace.

The name Noah is the same as the word for Grace reversed.

Often reversing a Hebrew word changes the meaning from good to evil but such is not the case with Noah. The only thing that is changed is the emphasis or order of two concepts embedded in the letters that are both positive.

The meaning of Grace is as follows:

Noon 50   **Chet** 8

LIFE SANCTUARY

GRACE IS A SANCTUARY THAT IS CREATED IN ORDER TO PRESERVE AND SUSTAIN LIFE.

Noah's name means Comfort. The concept of Comfort is as follows:

NOAH

Chet 8   **Noon** 50

LIFE HAS PROVIDED A SANCTUARY A PROVIDENTIAL PLACE OF REFUGE.

While the two concepts of Grace and Comfort are similar, they each have their own distinctives.

> ### GENESIS 5:29
> *And he called his name Noah, saying, This same shall **comfort** us concerning our work and toil of our hands, because of the ground which the Lord hath cursed.*

JOB • The Mystery Hidden in the Hebrew Pictures and Numbers

Now let's look at the picture and number meaning of "He Shall Comfort."

Notice that embedded in the Hebrew word "He Shall Comfort" is the word Grace.

Vav   Noon   Mem   Chet   Noon   Yood

Pictorial Meaning of "He Shall Comfort or Console."

⌐	YOOD	To work, a mighty deed, to make	Hand
~	NOON	Activity, life	Fish
Ⅲ	CHET	Private, to separate, fence, inner room	Sanctuary
ש	MEM	Liquid, massive, chaos	Water
~	NOON	Activity, life	Fish
٦	VAV	Add, to secure, wooden hook, wooden peg	Iron Nail

Pictorial Translation of "He Shall Comfort or Console."

Yood a mighty deed Noon to preserve life Chet in a sanctuary prepared to preserve and protect Mem from chaos and confusion. Noon Vav Securing Life!

Summary Messianic Meaning

God has ordained a Divine Deed in order to reverse the curse that has resulted in chaos, confusion and death. When that deed is accomplished, it will Secure Life!

You need to ask yourself the following question.

Did Job's "comforters" do any of the above?

Or were they simply playing their role as surrogate accusers?

What Might Have Been

Have you ever wondered what might have been the counsel of three Godly comforters? Imagine three comforters that had also experienced tribulation and seemingly unwarranted trials and sorrows.

What might they have said to Job?

We need not wonder, as we reach into the future to find three comforters whose words have been recorded in Holy Scripture.

Consider Joseph, the Favorite Son of Israel

Joseph, the son who suffered the slings and arrows of insult from his brothers, endured slavery and false slanderous accusations against his character, patiently endured prison and was finally elevated by the Lord to be second in charge of Egypt in order that many be saved including ALL the house of Israel.

What counsel would Righteous Joseph give to Job?

We find the answer in Genesis 50:20-21:

> ²⁰But as for you,
> *ye thought evil against me;*
> *but God meant it unto good,*
> to bring to pass, as it is this day,
> to save much people alive.
> ²¹Now therefore fear ye not:
> I will nourish you, and your little ones.
> And he comforted them,
> and spake kindly unto them.

We can imagine that Joseph's counsel to Job would be as follows:

Job, be comforted because perhaps the evil that has come upon you is meant for your good.

What Satan means for evil, God can transform into something good!

Enter, Isaiah the prophet.

The prophet that was literally sawn in half with a wooden saw was a testimony against the false prophets of Israel.

Isaiah was also a great man, highly esteemed that fell into disfavor with the enemies of God and suffered much for his faith, constancy and counsel.

What might Isaiah the prophet say to Job?

We find the answer in Isaiah 64:3-4:

> ³When thou didst terrible things
> which we looked not for,
> thou camest down,
> the mountains flowed down at thy presence.
> For since the beginning of the world
> men have not heard,
> nor perceived by the ear,
> neither hath the eye seen,
> O God, beside thee,
> what he hath prepared for him
> that waiteth for him.

In other words, the counsel of Isaiah to Job might have been as follows:

Job the trouble you're going through now, as terrible as it may seem, is nothing compared to what God has prepared for those that wait for Him.

Finally, Let's bring in the Apostle Paul

Paul suffered beatings and imprisonment.

The Apostle Paul was stoned once, shipwrecked three times, spent a day and a night adrift at sea, robbed, slandered by false friends and foes, suffered from hunger and thirst and was stripped naked and endured both heat and cold.

What counsel would the apostle Paul give to Job?

We find the answer in two places.

Paul would no doubt repeat the promise given by Isaiah with an added revelation that would have been a great comfort to anyone who truly loved the Lord and that certainly included Job.

We can read that encouraging promise made to the righteous in 1 Corinthians 2:5-10:

>⁵That your faith should not stand
>in the wisdom of men,
>but in the power of God.
>⁶Howbeit we speak wisdom among
>them that are perfect:
>yet not the wisdom of this world,
>nor of the princes of this world,
>that come to nought:
>⁷But we speak the wisdom of God in a mystery,
>even the hidden wisdom,
>which God ordained before the world unto our glory:
>⁸ Which none of the princes of this world knew:
>for had they known it,
>they would not have crucified the Lord of glory.
>**⁹ But as it is written,**
>**Eye hath not seen, nor ear heard,**
>**neither have entered into the heart of man,**
>**the things which God hath prepared**
>**for them that love him.**
>¹⁰ But God hath revealed them unto us by his Spirit:
>for the Spirit searcheth all things,
>yea, the deep things of God.

And there is no doubt that Paul, had he been summoned from the future to counsel Job, would have revealed the unfathomable wisdom of God disclosed in Romans 8:14-18:

> For as many as are led by the Spirit of God, they are the sons of God. ¹⁵For ye have not received the spirit of bondage again to fear; but ye have received the Spirit of adoption, whereby we cry, Abba, Father. ¹⁶The Spirit itself beareth witness with our spirit, that we are the children of God: ¹⁷And if children, then heirs; heirs of God, and joint-heirs with Christ; **if so be that we suffer with him, that we may be also glorified together.** ¹⁸For I reckon that the sufferings of this present time are not worthy to be compared with the glory which shall be revealed in us.

In conclusion, the Apostle Paul would have comforted Job with the following promise revealed in Romans 8:27-28:

> *And he that searcheth the hearts knoweth what is the mind of the Spirit, because he maketh intercession for the saints according to the will of God.* **And we know that all things work together for good to them that love God, to them who are the called according to his purpose.**

It is at the apex of a trial, the point where everything that could go wrong has gone wrong that the comfort that comes from the promises of God are most needed.

It is also the point at which those very promises are most often scorned.

This is the time when the curtain goes up and the true nature of the heart of man is exposed. You would think that at the time when sorrows overwhelm hope and all seems lost that a sure promise from God would be a welcome friend.

If you think that is the norm in today's Christians, then you are sadly mistaken.

The time of deepest trouble is most often when those that profess faith and confidence in God are exposed as the fair-weather friends of God that they really are.

I have been to enough Christian funerals and heard the hard words and opinions that sorrow reveals.

Bitterness at the unwelcome circumstance expressed by loved ones who would curse you to your face if you dared recite one of the promises of God.

I have heard those that would call themselves "Christians" counsel others not to "spout pious platitudes" like "all things work together for good" at a time of grief and loss.

Are you surprised?

You shouldn't be.

The heart of man is desperately wicked and crowded in every corner as it were with a mob of doubters and unbelievers who take any loss or disruption as a sign to run riot over all true religion.

Job's wife was not spared the sorrows and loss. Her sorrow did not include the added burden of physical affliction, but make no mistake she was suffering right along with Job.

Job's wife had been surrounded by every luxury available during the age she lived. She was no doubt happy and secure behind the hedge of God's protection and enjoyed all the benefits and privileges of a believer's wife.

Her faith was also put on trial and was found to be non-existent.

Job's misguided and miserable friends were stalwart compared to Job's unbelieving wife. Her counsel to her husband was swift and unsympathetic. She did not deliberate on the matter; she simply erupted with a stinging rebuke that must have cut Job to his heart.

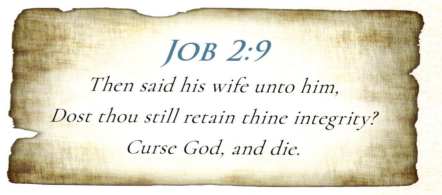

JOB 2:9
Then said his wife unto him,
Dost thou still retain thine integrity?
Curse God, and die.

When Job's wife delivered that striking blow to her husband, hell itself must have erupted in shouts of victory. If the angels in Heaven rejoice every time a sinner repents and believes, then Hell's fallen angels can also be expected to rejoice when a man's best friend on this earth desires to bring her own husband down to the place where hope is permanently extinguished and the worm never dies.

Job's counterpunch to this unwelcome strike against his soul was quick and powerful.

Even at Job's lowest point, when reason was clouded by pain and suffering, he rejected the counsel of his sour and unbelieving wife and branded her counsel with the name it deserved. Foolish!

The first blow to the heart by Job's wife was to be followed by an unrelenting series of body blows that we see delivered and received over 29 chapters. Job's miserable friends relentlessly pursue and press hard the scandal and slander against both Job and God. Their words are a testimony to how reasonable a false theology can sound.

And just when you think it can get no worse. At the lowest point in Job's now miserable life, when Job himself is trembling with his own misunderstandings of the situation, wondering why God has seemingly abandoned him, he raises an anthem of hope that lifts the darkness.

Consider the confession of Resurrection and Redemption found in Job 19:25-27:

> *For I know that my redeemer liveth,*
> *and that he shall stand at the latter day upon the earth:*
> *26 And though after my skin worms destroy this body,*
> *yet in my flesh shall I see God:*
> *27 Whom I shall see for myself,*
> *and mine eyes shall behold,*
> *and not another;*
> *though my reins be consumed within me.*

144 Consider when this prophetic announcement is uttered.

If you did not know the order of events in the story of Job, you might well imagine that this triumphant proclamation would come as a benediction. It would seem to best follow the events that restored Job after the pain was gone and forgotten, replaced with a double blessing that included a long and prosperous life.

But it didn't!

In the middle of the worst, Job rises up as it were and says what he must have considered his last words. The words he wished to be remembered by because they were words tested by the fiery trials of life and could not be doubted or thought insincere.

This is Job's finest moment.

CHAPTER 11

THE REAL MEANING OF THE NAME OF JOB!

And now it is time to reveal the true meaning of the name of Job, the meaning that unmasks the reason and purpose for the book of Job.

IT IS ALL ABOUT HOME!

For some of you, the sound of HOME floods the memory with warm images that are pleasant and peaceful. Home - an island refuge. Home, where you are cherished and encouraged. Home - the haven of rest. Does the very thought of HOME tantalize your senses? Does Home conjure up sunny thoughts and familiar scents that provide serene sanctuary for your heart? Is Home the safe harbor for your soul?

For many others, the sound of Home curls up your mind. The very word HOME withers your soul as the churlish thoughts of HOME dredge up sordid and sullied memories of neglect, abuse and a thousand arrows flying in your direction each dipped in the venom of shame and disappointment, all aimed at your wounded heart.

For many here today, Home is a harbor of refuge. For many others, it's a battlefield wreaking with the stench of overwhelming discouragement. It's a place where memories are whipped up into a furious tempest that rushes through your once cherished dreams that have all been stripped of hope and purpose by the gloomy winds of chaos, resentment, betrayal and despair that swept through your HOME.

No matter where you find yourself on the spectrum, whether you came from a home that was happy or a Home filled with horrors, you will be forced to admit that even the most ideal home was far from perfect.

There is no perfect home on this earth because a home is made up of imperfect, flawed and sinful people.

So, while the tragedy of sin and its consequences may be more evident in the horrible home, it is still present in the happiest of homes.

The inescapable truth is that we all yearn for the **perfect home.**

The Lord is not unaware of this longing and desire since He is the one that put it into the heart of man. He is the one who created Home and everything it encompasses.

And so, we MIGHT ask the question.

Home...

How important is Home to you?

Or is there a more important question, a larger question we might want to ponder?

How important is Home to God?

Consider the drama that was planned in Heaven and is now in the final act, the last scene, and mere seconds on God's celestial clock from all coming to an abrupt and final end.

A drama started in a garden full of delights and free from sin and sorrow. Followed by the arrival of a stealthy enemy who cunningly deceived the matron of the Garden into doing the one thing, the only thing that would turn her perfect world upside down and result in her expulsion from her home in the Garden of Eden.

Eve was deceived into coveting with her gaze, then handling and finally eating of the forbidden fruit from the tree of the knowledge of good and evil. This deception resulted in a breach, a space so wide in the chasm between God's Heaven and earth where man dwelt that no man could heal or mend it. This earthquake in God's creation was followed minutes later by an even more grievous act of sedition, disloyalty, rebellion and betrayal.

Adam, the pinnacle of God's creation and the acting vice-regent of this earth, knowingly listened to the voice of the enemy that he knew had deceived Eve and instead of calling on the Lord for mediation joined his wife in the sumptuous bite that filled his soul with the deadly venom of chaos, confusion and death.

In one brief second with the clinching of the jaw, the deed was done, the harmony between Creator and Creature was breached, the friend of God who had been warned against listening to any voice besides the voice of his Heavenly father abandoned the loving relationship with his Creator in order to maintain his fellowship with the fellow creature God had created to be his helpmate.

In that one moment, Adam betrayed his heart as he loved another more than he loved his Heavenly Father.

Adam and Eve were expelled from their Home. They lost the physical location with all its wondrous bounty and benefits. More importantly, the one relationship that made Home, Home was discarded by Adam in one instant leaving both Adam and Eve HOMELESS.

If the ideal of Home was first demonstrated in the shadow type of the Garden of Eden, a real place that represented a rough figure of something even more glorious, tangible and eternal wouldn't you think that God the creator would have something to say about it.

Of course, God did have something to say about it.

Adam and Eve were driven out of the Garden of Eden as it was not a place prepared for imperfect sinners. Adam and Eve in their fallen state could have no expectation to continue to inhabit Eden's Garden, the shadow arch-type of home and were certainly disqualified from entering the eternal and infinitely more substantial Heavenly home that was to be inhabited by a sinless creature who possessed an unfeigned and overflowing love for their Sovereign Creator.

It seemed that in the moment of Adam's rebellion, HOME was transformed from a holy enterprise full of benefits to an unholy state of constant struggle, trouble, disappointment and sorrow.

So, whatever your best thoughts of Home may be, they are imperfect and marred. All the Rockwellian painting or Currier and Ives images of the ideal home cannot erase the truth of the matter, home is not what it was meant from the beginning to be. Not even close.

Time cannot erase all the bad memories of home no matter how rosy the lens through which you remember the good and forget the evil that encompassed your home on this earth.

Is this the final verdict on the Home?

Is there no hope for the repair of the Homes rocked by rebellion, groaning under the weight of abuse, driven to madness under the influence of drugs and alcohol, and suffering from the broken familial bonds that are so easily torn apart in this age of self-seeking indulgence and independence?

God, Himself has given us the answer to this question in the first book ever written.

Do you know what book that is?

We all know that Genesis is the first book in the Bible but it is not the oldest book in the Bible.

The oldest book in the Bible is tucked in between the book of Esther and the Psalms. It is the 18th book in the Bible and of the 66 books that are contained between the book of Genesis and Revelation, it is the 22nd longest book written.

What book am I talking about?

The Book of JOB.

Job was most likely born a generation or so before Abraham in the land of UZ.

Uz was the grandson of Shem, who was one of the three sons of Noah. It is very likely that the land of UZ was named after Noah's great-grandson.

The location of Uz is disputed. The most likely location, based on the facts presented in the Scriptural narrative is that UZ is east of the Sea of Galilee and south of Damascus. Today, this is the area we know as western Jordan.

When we read the first verse in the book of Job what do we learn?

> ## JOB 1:1
> There was a man in the land of Uz, whose name was Job; and that man was perfect and upright, and one that feared God, and eschewed evil.

The first thing the Spirit of God, the unseen mover and editor of all the books of the Bible, notices is that Job is Righteous.

JOB is identified as the most righteous man in the east by none other than God Himself.

The second thing we learn is that Job had a big family.

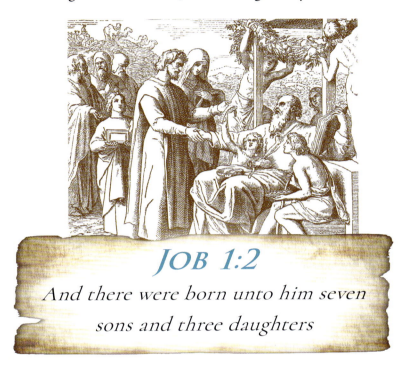

JOB 1:2
And there were born unto him seven sons and three daughters

Job was not only righteous, and the father of a large family, Job was RICH.

JOB 1:3
His substance also was seven thousand sheep, and three thousand camels, and five hundred yoke of oxen, and five hundred she asses, and a very great household; so that this man was the greatest of all the men of the east.

152

The next two verses are the key to understanding the entire book of Job. You see, there is a mystery hidden in the book of JOB and it is all about something that was dear to the heart of JOB.

With all his status, wealth and wisdom, Job had a constant nagging concern that continually vexed him.

Listen to what is revealed in the opening stanza of the book of Job.

JOB 1:4-5

4 And his sons went and feasted in their houses, every one his day; and sent and called for their three sisters to eat and to drink with them. 5 And it was so, when the days of their feasting were gone about, that Job sent and sanctified them, and rose up early in the morning, and offered burnt offerings according to the number of them all: for Job said, **It may be that my sons have sinned, and cursed God in their hearts.** *Thus did Job continually.*

I want you to notice that these were days of feasting. These feasts included eating and drinking wine and took place seven times a year.

JOB • The Mystery Hidden in the Hebrew Pictures and Numbers

How long were these celebrations?

We are not told, but all the clues point to an extended period of time.

Perhaps three or four days, perhaps a week, and perhaps longer.

The Scriptures do not indicate that these feasts were sinful in themselves. There is no hint that anything untoward was happening during these feasts and yet father Job was so concerned about what they had become or might lead to that he devoted himself to the role of a mediator on behalf of his sons and daughters whenever they took place.

Job was a man, who we are told, shunned every evil thing and so we can be certain that Job's concerns for his family were not without warrant.

While his family was feasting, eating and drinking, Job was praying for each one of them continually. Job was offering sacrifices on their behalf and beseeching Heaven to sanctify his sons and daughters.

What was his overriding concern?

Was Job concerned that his sons might mismanage their great wealth?

No!

Was he concerned that they might not be making the kind of decisions that would get ahead in this world?

No!

Was Job concerned about their health?

No?

Was Job concerned that they were not paying enough attention to maintaining their flocks and herds?

No?

So, just exactly what was Job concerned about?

Job was concerned that they might sin and curse God in their hearts.

Job prayed for his children without concern for his time or comfort.

If his children were tempted by the worldly pleasures, comforts and sumptuous culinary delights of this world as a regular routine of their life then Job would spend that same amount of time interceding, praying, and petitioning His Heavenly Father and offering sacrifices for his children.

This must have pleased God very much since God announced in the courts of Heaven that there was no one equal to JOB in righteous living.

Job's heart was an open book to the Lord, who knows all the secrets hidden from all others, and God saw that Job truly hated Evil.

Job was a man with a heart that was in harmony with the heart of God.

The story of Job takes a jarring and abrupt turn for the worse when Satan is allowed to first take away everything that Job owns including the one thing that Job could never replace, his family, the very family that he had been so diligently praying for was consumed in a fiery tempest that came down from the Heavens.

Finally, Job himself was ravaged by Satan.

Let's examine the Picture meaning of the name JOB one more time as we look again at the Hebrew word composed of:

∀	**ALEPH**	Aleph pictured as the Ox, The Strong Leader
⌐	**YOOD**	Pictured as the Hand doing a deed
ף	**VAV**	Pictured as the Iron Nail that fastens and secures two things together
⊐	**BEYT**	And finally, Beyt pictured as a Tent or House

These are the four Hebrew Pictograms that compose the picture meaning of the name of JOB. As you consider these pictures, what comes to mind?

Can you discover the Messianic message in the Pictures embedded in the name of Job?

156

Consider a startling message delivered by the Messiah thousands of years after the time of Job.

This message that echoes the meaning hidden in the name of Job is recorded in the Gospel of John chapter 14 verses two and three.

Listen to the words of Jesus as He comforts His disciples just before He leaves them to return to His home in Heaven. Jesus said:

> ### John 14:2-3
> In my Father's house are many mansions:
> if it were not so, I would have told you.
> I go to prepare a place for you.
>
> And if I go and prepare a place for you,
> I will come again, and receive you unto myself;
> that where I am, there ye may be also.

JOB

Beyt — 2　　Vav — 6　　Yood — 10　　Aleph — 1

JOB • The Mystery Hidden in the Hebrew Pictures and Numbers

Now, look at the promise hidden in plain sight in the name of JOB.

	ALEPH	God the Father is going to
	YOOD	Accomplish a mighty deed ordained in Heaven
	VAV	In order to secure for man
	BEYT	A Heavenly home that is fashioned by the Son of God

Obviously, the message is clear enough but we must wonder how this miracle is possible.

How are imperfect sinners once at enmity with God suddenly welcomed into God's perfect household?

The answer is found in the middle of the name of Job.

The first thing you need to notice is that this message is surrounded by an Aleph and a Beyt , the first and last Hebrew letters in the name of Job.

JOB

Why is this important?

Aleph ⟁ is not only the first letter in the name of Job, it is the first letter in the Hebrew Aleph-Beyt. It is the also the number 1 and represents God the Father.

Beyt ⌐⌐ is the last letter in the name of Job, it is the second letter in the Hebrew Aleph-Beyt. Beyt ⌐⌐ is also the number 2 and represents God the Son.

Do you see the message in the first and last letters in the name of Job?

The Aleph ⟁ and the Beyt ⌐⌐ is a picture of the FATHER, Aleph ⟁ Beyt ⌐⌐ that includes Beyt ⌐⌐ the SON.

Between the Aleph ⟁ and the Beyt ⌐⌐; between God the Father and God the Son is a revelation for all mankind hidden in the name of Job.

God the Father is represented by the Number 1 ⟁ and He is the one that initiates the plan to bridge the gap and heal the breach that separates Man from his Heavenly Father.

God the Son represented by the Number 2 is the one that accomplishes the Father's plan to save mankind.

The mystery of the name of Job contains a promise.

Job's name promises a home in Heaven. This promise is surrounded by the Aleph and the Beyt.

ALEPH		God the Father is the one who initiates and plans.
BEYT		God the Son is the one that accomplishes.

The question is what was initiated by God the Father and accomplished by God the Son?

The answer can be found in the two letters in the middle of Job's name.

What do you suppose the two letters in the middle reveal?

The two letters in the middle of the name of Job are the Yood and the Vav.

Let's look at What is in the Middle

The Mystery Hidden in the Hebrew Pictures and Numbers • JOB

160

What is in the middle of Job's name that gives us hope that God the Father is going to secure a place in Heaven for sinful man?

The answer is found in YOOD ˡ↙, the number 10.

Ten ˡ↙ is one of four Sacred Numbers that means Ordinal Perfection.

What does the number 10 ˡ↙, Ordinal Perfection, mean?

In a nutshell, Ordinal Perfection, the number 10 ˡ↙, means that God has ordained a plan in Heaven that will unfold on earth in order to accomplish God's Divine will.

It is not a surprise then that the Sacred name of God YHVH begins with the Sacred Number 10 ˡ↙, the Hebrew letter Yood ˡ↙ that is pictured as a Hand doing a Divine Deed.

What does Yood tell us?

Yood ˡ↙, the number 10 ˡ↙, tells us that God has a plan, a Divine plan for men and women that love Him.

So, what have we learned?

We have learned that the transportation of Man from earth to Heaven, where we go to be with God the Father to live as an adopted member of the family of God in a place prepared by God the Son, is all based on a PLAN of GOD.

Notice again that it is a Plan that Secures for us this amazing Heavenly destiny.

Next to the Yood ˡ↙ pictured as a Hand and the number TEN ˡ↙ we see the Hebrew letter Vav.

Vav is pictured as the Iron nail and is also the number 6, the number of man. Do you see the symbol of the Iron Nail as it makes a connection or attachment on behalf of sinful man?

Is our Eternal destiny secured by an Iron Nail?

It takes little imagination to see the Messianic significance of VAV ו the letter that secures for us the promise found in the name of JOB. The promise echoed by the Savior Himself just before He went back to His kingdom in Heaven. The promise that God the Father is going to secure a home for us that has been prepared by God the Son.

Mention an Iron Nail ו in reference to God's plan for man and how the Son of God accomplished the Father's will and what comes to mind?

If you're trusting in Christ, what comes to mind is that you and I are on the reserved guest list for an apartment in Heaven and all because of the plan of God that has as one of its revelations a small seemingly unimportant Iron Nail ו.

The Iron Nail ו. What a bittersweet vision it unfolds before us.

The secret to understanding the Messianic message in the name of JOB.

Job, the man who declared this prophecy to be true as recorded in the book of Job.

JOB 19:25-26

For I know that my redeemer liveth, and that he shall stand at the latter day upon the earth:

²⁶ And though after my skin worms destroy this body, yet in my flesh shall I see God:

162

Job, who believed in the resurrection of and the LIFE secured by a Savior, has the mystery of the means of that security and sure hope hidden in the THIRD letter ◌ of his own name.

Our Savior willingly grasped the iron nail ◌ in order that one day we might, along with Job, see our Savior face to face and be swept gloriously into His household to be with Him forever.

Have you looked up and seen the Savior secured to the wooden cross?

Have you trusted in Him and Him alone for your complete salvation?

Have your sins been covered by the perfect and precious blood of Yeshua?

If you have, then you can take great comfort in the fact that Job is now your middle name.

Receive the free gift of God's Salvation. Simply look to the Cross and see your Savior, cast all your sins upon Him, trust His as the only substitutionary atonement that will be received as a perfect sacrifice by God the Father and you will one day live in a perfect Heaven having been both cleansed and glorified by a perfect Savior who joyfully came to earth in order that you might be Saved.

1 ◌ God, the Father 10 ◌ is going to accomplish a deed ordained in Heaven in order 6 ◌ to secure for Job 2 ◌ a Heavenly Home that has been Prepared by the Son of God.

CHAPTER 12
GOD'S MYSTERY MIRACLE MATH

The prophecy in the name of Job was meant for Heaven not earth. Job may not have understood the prophecy in his name but his heart revealed that the prophecy would be regarded as Job's Blessed Hope.

JOB may have given up on living in this world but he would never abandon the only faith that is pleasing to God.

Job was looking for a Heavenly home.

What Job did not realize is that God had not only given Job a prophecy in his name, he was about to be given a miraculous sign so that not only Job but also you and me might know that the prophecy was true.

A sign that as beyond anything Job could have imagined. A sign that is stamped with God's math, which Job would immediately comprehend.

Now consider the promise made in the name of Job. Let's personalize the promise.

(1) God the Father **(10)** is going to accomplish a deed ordained in Heaven in order **(6)** to secure for JOB **(2)** a Heavenly home that is fashioned by the Son of God

JOB 42:10-12
And the Lord turned the captivity of Job, when he prayed for his friends: **also the Lord gave Job twice as much as he had before.**

> Then came there unto him all his brethren, and all his sisters, and all they that had been of his acquaintance before, and did eat bread with him in his house: and they bemoaned him, and comforted him over all the evil that the Lord had brought upon him: every man also gave him a piece of money, and every one an earring of gold.
>
> So, the Lord blessed the latter end of Job more than his beginning: for he had fourteen thousand sheep, and six thousand camels, and a thousand yoke of oxen, and a thousand female donkeys.

And now for the verse that reveals the one blessing that must have given Job more joy and comfort than all the other double blessings combined.

Let's look at the Hebrew word for Bless.

BLESS

Kaf 20   Reysh 200   Beyt 2

Letters are right to left, original Hebrew.

JOB • The Mystery Hidden in the Hebrew Pictures and Numbers

CONVENTIONAL USAGE OF
BLESS

The dictionary defines the word bless as "to consecrate or sanctify by a religious rite; make or pronounce holy."

Another meaning of bless is to request of God the bestowal of divine favor on a person, place or thing. It also means to extol as holy and to glorify.

FIRST USE OF HEBREW WORD
BLESS
IN SCRIPTURES

> **GENESIS 12:3**
> *And I will bless them that bless thee, and curse him that curseth thee: and in thee shall all families of the earth be blessed.*

It is interesting that the first time the word bless is used in the Scriptures it is in relationship to Abraham, the one to whom the promises were made. The promises were made to Abraham and his descendants. And it was from Abraham that the genealogical progression that would gloriously conclude in the coming of the promised Messiah.

Messiah was destined to make atonement for fallen and sinful Mankind. The blessing given to Abraham would have its final and ideal fulfillment in the salvation of the world. Keep this in mind as we discover the amazing picture that is embedded in the Hebrew word translated into English as bless! You can read about this unconditional promise in the book of Genesis chapters 22:17-18.

THE PICTURE OF BLESS

BLESS

KAF REYSH BEYT
20 200 2

BE-RACH

The Picture Meaning of Bless

HOUSE
BEYT

House – Tent – Son – Family – Dwelling Place – The Physical Tent/Body – Inside – Within – First Letter in the Torah that Identifies the Son of God

PRINCE
REYSH

A Person – The Head – The Highest – The Sum – The Supreme – The First – The Most Important – The Top – Master – Leader – Prince – Head

ATONEMENT
KAF

To Cover – To Open – To Allow – Atonement – Palm

Picture Translation of Bless

Beyt Reysh is the Son. The Son in view as we discover the ideal picture meaning embedded in the three Hebrew letters is the Son who is the Prince of Heaven who is coming to make Atonement. He is coming to cover the sin that keeps us from fellowship with our Heavenly Father.

The Number Meaning of Bless

BLESS

KAF REYSH BEYT
20   200   2

God the Son

Difference – Good or Evil – Division – Living Word – Second – Second Person of the Godhead – To Come Alongside to Hinder – To Come Alongside for Help – God the Son

REYSH 200
SUFFICIENCY OF GOD

ADEQUACY OF THE ETERNAL – MULTIPLIED ORDINAL PERFECTION – SUFFICIENCY TO ACCOMPLISH A PURPOSE – RANSOM THAT IS BOTH EFFICIENT AND SUFFICIENT TO ACCOMPLISH REDEMPTION – SUFFICIENCY OF GOD IN THE FACE OF MAN'S INSUFFICIENCY

KAF 20
REDEMPTION

CONCENTRATED MEANING OF ORDINAL PERFECTION (2 X 10) – EXPECTANCY

THE NUMBER TRANSLATION OF BLESS

The Hebrew word Bless is crowned with the number 2. Clearly the Son of God, the second person in the Divine trinity is in view.

The Mission is also summarized in the exponential meaning infused into the number two that has the biblical significance of announcing both Redemption and Atonement.

The translation is simple.

God the Son is the only one Sufficient to Redeem Mankind!

The Mystery Hidden in the Hebrew Pictures and Numbers • JOB

> ## ROMANS 4:7
> *Saying, Blessed are they whose iniquities are forgiven, and whose sins are covered.*

Read what it says in Job 42:12:

> *So, the Lord blessed the latter end of Job more than his beginning: for he had fourteen thousand sheep, and six thousand camels, and a thousand yoke of oxen, and a thousand female donkeys.*

Now ask yourself what the ultimate blessing is?

You might be blessed with Wealth. Is the ideal meaning of Bless connected to Wealth?

You might be blessed with Health. Is the ideal meaning of Bless connected to Health?

You might be blessed with Prestige. Is the ideal meaning of Bless connected to Prominence and Prestige?

You might be blessed with Longevity. Is the ideal meaning of Bless connected to Long Life?

Or is it something else?

The Messianic Meaning of the Pictures and Numbers gives us the answer.

What is the picture and number portrait of the Hebrew word Bless or Blessing?

The picture and numbers reveal the answer.

To be blessed is to have a HOME in Heaven that has been secured for you by the Atonement for sin made on your behalf by the Son of God, the Prince of Heaven.

Notice that the Hebrew word we translate as Bless is Crowned with the number TWO.

I would like to notice the number 20 that is also the Hebrew letter Kaf .

It is not an accident that the number 20 is the number of Salvation.

What does any of this have to do with Job?

The answer is in the math.

Ask yourself how many children Job had in the end?

We know that he started out with 7 sons and 3 daughters.

> **JOB 1:2**
> *And there were born unto him seven sons and three daughters*

Everything that Job had before his trial was doubled in this life.

7000 sheep were doubled and replaced with 14,000.

3000 camels were doubled and replaced with 6000.

500 yoke of Oxen were doubled and replaced with 1000.

500 female donkeys were doubled and replaced with 1000.

And so on and so on until we get to the 10 children that were murdered by Satan.

Notice that Job was not given 20 children after the loss of the ten.

Job was given 10 more children, 7 boys and 3 girls

Everything was doubled except for one thing.

In the first chapter of Job we are given an insight that provides one of the clues regarding the mystery of the double blessing given to Job at the end of his trial.

> ### Job 1:5
> When the days of feasting had completed their cycle,
> Job would send and consecrate them,
> rising up early in the morning
> and offering burnt offerings
> according to the number of them all;
> for Job said,
> **"Perhaps my sons have sinned and cursed God in their hearts."**
> Thus, Job did continually.

Job's greatest concern in this life was for the spiritual life of his children.

When Job's children were lost to him it must have been a double tragedy. Losing your sons and daughters tragically in this life is horrible. The thought that they were lost to him throughout eternity was the very thought that kept Job on his knees as it were, constantly praying for their eternal souls.

There are a number of themes that run through the story of Job.

Clearly, Job was troubled and vexed by the loss of his children. As Job was being tested and tried in the fiery furnace of tribulation only one question must have gnawed at his soul.

What was the final destiny of his 10 children?

Job could no longer pray for them as they had been cast into eternity.

Where did they go?

Where they in anguish or in glory?

Job will not need to wait until he himself entered into the eternal city of God to find out what happened to his beloved children.

God gives Job a math problem that answers the question that is on Job's mind.

God says to Job,

"Whatever you had JOB I will double it!"

Twice as many sheep, camels, oxen, and donkeys.

Double the wealth, double the servants to manage the overflowing bounty and double the number of blest children.

But only 10 children were added at the end of the trial.

Where are the other 10 children?

Job understood the mystery of God's Grace Math and his heart must have leapt with joy as he considered the revelation God granted him in the **Miracle of the Doubling.**

The ten children at the beginning of the trial were taken from this life to live in the eternal home of the Heavenly Father.

Instead of 10 blest children, Job is given 20 children secured by the Heavenly Father as a result of a Divine Deed ordained in Heaven and carried out in a way none could ever imagine in this life.

The story of Job is not primarily about perseverance or patience.

The story of Job is about hanging onto the promises of God for your dear life because in the end those promises are the only hope of eternal life.

God's promise is for you, and for all those that love the Lord.

And now you understand how the meaning of the name of Job is miraculously demonstrated in the life of Job and his family.

The mystery in the name of Job has a Messianic meaning that we now understand. The Vav ו that secures for us a Heavenly dwelling place is the same iron nail ו that secured our Savior's hand to the Cross of Calvary.

Put your confidence in the finished work of Jesus the Christ and you will live eternally in the home that He has prepared for you in Heaven.

The Mystery of Job Revealed!

∀	**ALEPH**	Our Loving Heavenly Father
┘	**YOOD**	Has planned and purposed a Mighty Deed that will be accomplished at the Appointed Time on the earth
٦	**VAV**	That will Secure our Salvation, Atonement and Redemption
⊏	**BEYT**	In order that we might enter our Heavenly Home.

A home prepared for Job and his family, a home for all those that love God and have been Redeemed by the Precious Blood of Jesus the Christ!

In Conclusion

Our first introduction to Job on the earth is the start point from which this entire revelation must be understood. It is the lens through which the mystery of Job is revealed.

Consider what Job was doing when we first met him.

Job was praying for his 10 children.

Why?

Because he saw a pattern in their lives that was going to lead to a pathway that would find its conclusion in death and destruction. A pathway that Job saw with spiritual eyes as evidenced by his prayer. Job was given a glimpse of what God saw being manifest on the earth in the lives of Job's children.

And what is that?

The condition of the Human Heart!

Job, the perfect earthly father, was concerned that the lifestyle of his children was going to lead to stony hearts so engrossed in the pleasures of this life that they would one day CURSE GOD!

Job was concerned about his children's eternity.

While they "played" Job "prayed."

The story of Job is the story of answered prayer.

Prayers not answered in the way Job expected. Answered in a way that is a surprise that goes over the heads of most readers including most Christians.

God used Satan as an instrument to answer Job's prayer.

But how can that be? Satan is only interested in stealing, killing and destroying. How can God use that?

The story of Job answers this longstanding question that is still asked to this day.

"Where is God in this personal disaster?"

"If God was a loving caring God then why did this or that tragedy happen?"

Left to their own devices, the 10 children of Job were headed toward the doorway that would lead to death. They would have been Satan's prize.

God used Satan to answer the prayer of Job as regards to the most pressing matter on Job's mind. Job's prayer is the prayer of every Godly father on the earth.

Do you hear Job's anguished cry?

Do you understand why he was praying while his children were eating and drinking?

When impatient and impetuous Satan took the physical lives of the 10 children of Job it seemed that all was lost and that Satan had won.

But he hadn't!

Had he left the children to their own devices they would have one day been ensnared by the cares of this world and under the power of the prince of darkness.

What Satan meant for evil, God meant for good.

God's mysterious math opened up the revelation that brought Job the answer to his longstanding and persistent prayers for his children.

His children were robbed of a long and prosperous life on this earth in order that they might be delivered from the doorway that God and Job both knew was on their near horizon. They were taken out of this world in order that they might be saved from the tragedy of forsaking God and cursing Him in their hearts.

Job's kids were now safeguarded in Heaven where Job would one day be reunited with the original ten and the ten that followed the promise of a double blessing that can only be understood in light of the mystery math of God's Grace.

Trust God and LIVE!

And now you know the true mystery and meaning of the book of Job!

CHECK OUT OUR WEBSITE FOR OTHER TITLES!

www.lighthouse.pub

Author and editor C.J. Lovik spins a spectacular story of a family at the turn of the 20th century, full of adventure, mystery, life lessons, and solid biblical teachings. The mysteries surrounding Heaven are carefully revealed in both the plain text of Scripture and then amplified by the skillful unfolding of allegories. Those who read this book will understand more about Heaven.

Are you trapped in a prison of addiction or an unhealthy relationship? Have you been a victim of an empty religious experience that promised you rest? If so, you have found yourself in a snare set by Satan that promised rest but ended in a darkness that has robbed you of hope. Call on the name of Jesus and ask for freedom from your prison, and you will find rest.

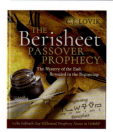

Explore the very first prophecy found in the Bible, just waiting to be discovered, right in the very first word of the Bible. Is this a prophecy which has been sealed up, just waiting to be unfolded at the end of the age? Has God revealed the end in the beginning? Join author C.J. Lovik as he explores one of the most ancient of prophecies.

From the editor of the critically acclaimed and recently republished Pilgrim's Progress, author and editor C.J. Lovik brings a unique contribution to the retelling of this classic tale. Lovik brings a fresh and unique view, allowing for a modern audience to read and understand, yet preserving the deep and beloved truths of Bunyan's timeless tale.

www.lighthouse.pub

Visit our website to purchase books, DVDs, and other Christ-centered media, and to preview upcoming titles.

Explore the majesty of the
Old Testament Scriptures
with these resources

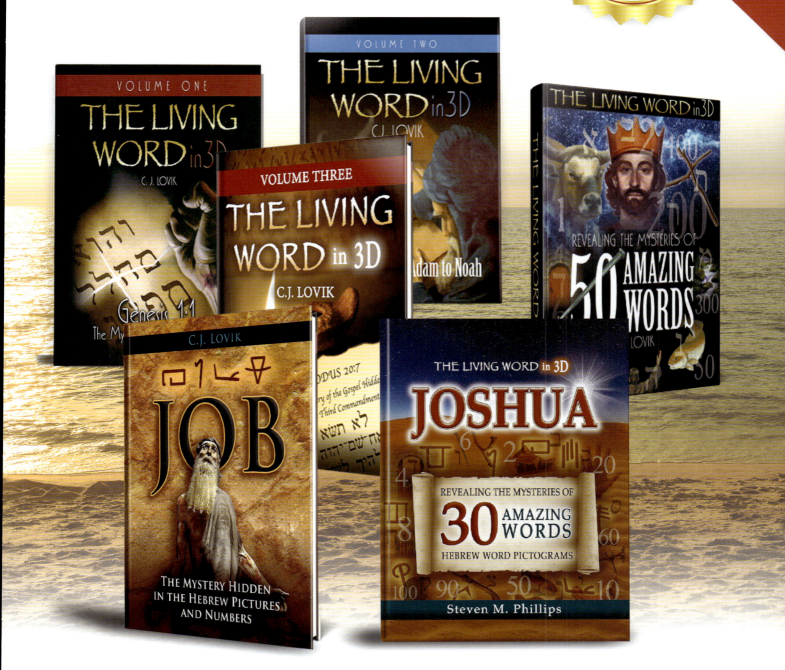

"Lord reveal yourself to me!" - C.J. Lovik, The Living Word in 3D

www.lighthouse.pub